D1114785

This special edition of *Ray Miller's Houston*
is limited to three hundred copies.
The book was set by Sandra Mahon Kana
in Century Book type.
Capital Printing, Inc., printed the book in color
and black and white on
70-pound Consolidated Frostbrite Matte,
80-pound Productolith Gloss
and 24-pound Champion Carnival Kraft paper.
The color photographs were made by Fred Edison.
Color separations were made by
American Color Corporation.
The text was bound and cases were made by
Universal Custom Products, Inc., using
Holliston Roxite Cloth.
The book was designed by John Hillenbrand.

This is copy number

215

Books by Ray Miller

Eyes of Texas Travel Guide: Panhandle/Plains Edition
Eyes of Texas Travel Guide: Fort Worth/Brazos Valley Edition
Eyes of Texas Travel Guide: Hill Country/Permian Basin Edition
Eyes of Texas Travel Guide: San Antonio/Border Edition
Eyes of Texas Travel Guide: Dallas/East Texas Edition
Eyes of Texas Travel Guide: Houston/Gulf Coast Edition

Ray Miller's Houston

RAY MILLER'S
HOUSTON

Copyright© 1982 by Ray Miller

All rights reserved under International and Pan-American
Copyright Conventions. Published in the United States
by Cordovan Press, a Division of Cordovan Corporation.
FIRST EDITION

Library of Congress Catalog Card Number: 82-73284
ISBN: 0-89123-025-4

Design: John Hillenbrand

Production art: Ginny Bliss

Set in Century Book by Sandra Mahon Kana
Printed in the United States of America
by Capital Printing, Austin

To Gray and Geoff

CONTENTS

FOREWORD

It has been my privilege to know Ray Miller and to follow his career from the time he was a fledgling reporter. He has escalated to great heights in his profession. More than once I have heard young radio and television reporters refer to him as their idol.

Instead of retiring to an easy life of inactivity when he completed his tenure with KPRC, he chose to visit many parts of Texas to record and report on some of the unique glories of our state. He is owed much for perpetuating in his *Eyes of Texas Travel Guides* these captivating, historical sagas.

Now in this volume, Mr. Miller returns to the city of his love — a city he has seen grow, develop and prosper. There is no one better qualified to give us the overview contained in this book, and to furnish an insight into Houston as it has been and is, than this gifted author.

Leon Jaworski

INTRODUCTION

It may be presumptuous of me to write a book about a city many people know better than I do. The institutions that give Houston most of its strength were established well before I came here in 1939. The port had already eclipsed Galveston. The refinery complex was already impressive. Experts already were predicting most of what has happened since. But I have had a ringside seat most of the time I have been here. I have worked as a reporter, photographer and editor and as a producer of radio and television news programs all the time except for a period of military service.

I discovered in the course of developing "The Eyes of Texas" television program that a great many people share my interest in how Texas and Texans got the way they are. This discovery led me to write six books about various sections of the state. They are travel guides with a little history worked in. This book is less a guide and more a history, with some personal observations and reminiscences.

It probably is presumptuous, but I have done it anyway.

Ray Miller
Houston
July, 1982

PART ONE

Some Personal Experiences
Color Photographs

"Houston may be short on history, but it is long on a lot of other things people admire — like guts, vitality, prosperity and the freedom and imagination to keep an eye on tomorrow."

Geraldo Rivera, ABC-TV News, 1981

People come to Houston now from everywhere and for all kinds of reasons. Time was when most of the people moving to Houston came from smaller cities and often with the idea of moving on later to a bigger city. This idea is not as prevalent or as valid as it once was. The list of cities bigger than Houston is shrinking; the list of liveable bigger cities is very, very short.

Jack McGrew of Radio Station KPRC offered me a better job in 1939 than the one I had at KFJZ in Fort Worth. I accepted the offer without ever thinking much about whether I wanted to live in Houston. I was sure I would get better offers later and eventually take H.V. Kaltenborn's place in New York. I could endure Houston in the meantime.

My first impression of the city was that it was bigger than Fort Worth without being more of a city. Houston seemed disorderly and unfinished and full of people from somewhere else. Fort Worth had alleys where people put their trash and garbage until it could be picked up. Houston people piled their trash and garbage up at the front curb. People told me it was because developers controlled Houston and developers didn't like to waste land on alleys.

Buses had replaced the street cars, but the service was not good even then. The streets were littered and they were rough. I had never seen land so flat before. I had never seen so much rain. The first time I saw the streets all flooded I thought it was a big news story. I got used to the flooded streets and the cockroaches and the mosquitos and I was getting used to the humidity when air conditioning came

Houston was just an overgrown town at the end of the 1930s. Street cars had only recently stopped running on Main Street. Parking was still permitted on both sides of the street. The population was 384,000. The tallest building was the Gulf Building with 35 floors (illuminated tower, center).

along and made it less of a problem.

William Goyen has written that he never felt he belonged here. It seemed to him that the people he knew when he was growing up in Woodland Heights all longed to be back in the smaller towns they came from. I know the feeling. I still thought of Fort Worth as home at first. I am not sure exactly when this changed, but gradually I came to feel that the disarray in Houston was a creative disarray. Houston was on its way to becoming something Fort Worth would never be. Houston was busy putting first things first and there seemed an implied promise that when it was all built, somebody would tidy it up.

Whatever had to be done always had been done and, therefore, it always would be. I began to believe that. I believed it for a long time before I learned that a small group of powerful men had assumed the responsibility for spotting obstacles and finding ways around them. These bankers, financiers and oil millionaires started meeting informally in Suite 8-F at the Lamar Hotel in the 1930s to talk about ways to advance Houston's interests. One of the founding members of the 8-F group was George R. Brown of Brown and Root. He once described his purpose this way: "We must look a long way down the road and plan the future needs of the city to insure that Houston never strangles itself in its own growth — that expansion is never halted by lack of space and utilities." Houston's growth never was planned in the usual sense. It occurred because powerful Houstonians saw to it that nothing happened to prevent it. I didn't know this at the time, but the optimism was contagious and I caught it.

I had lived in Houston less than two years when the Naval Reserve called me to active duty for World War II. But when anyone in the Navy asked me where I came from, I always said, "Houston." I was a convert. I seldom thought again about getting better offers in bigger cities. I was sure Houston was going to be big enough for me.

Downtown Houston dies after dark these days, but there was life after dark downtown before World War II and for a few years afterward. There were four major movie

Above: *The Lamar Hotel has been the meeting place of Houston's leading movers and shakers since the early 1930s. They discuss the city's problems and opportunities and the merits of various political candidates in Suite 8-F. Jesse Jones built the Lamar in 1927 on the corner of Main and Lamar, where he had previously operated a lumberyard. Jones lived on the top floor of the hotel.*

Below: *The hosts for the meetings in Suite 8-F are George R. Brown and the Brown and Root Company. Brown and Root was founded in 1919 by Herman Brown and Dan Root. George Brown became a partner in 1923. He was Herman Brown's younger brother. Root died in 1929. Herman Brown died in 1962. Brown and Root has been a subsidiary of the Halliburton Company since 1962.*

houses downtown. There were dining and dancing in the Empire Room at the Rice Hotel for the well-to-do and perky carhops to serve hamburgers to the rest of us at Prince's Drive-Ins. I managed to grow up in Fort Worth without being exposed to oysters on the half shell. I discovered raw oysters at Tony Massa's original oyster bar at Louisiana and Capitol, where the Civic Center Plaza is today. My sons and I have had a custom for years of feasting on Massa's oysters the Saturday before Christmas. Tony is dead, but his

Left: *The two biggest movie houses in Houston were Loew's and the Metropolitan, side by side in the 1000 block of Main Street next to the Lamar Hotel. The Kirby was less than a block away in the 900 block. All three were demolished in the 1960s and 70s.*

Above: *A showman named Doug Prince ran the biggest hamburger business in town in the 30s and for many years afterward. This was Prince's Drive-In on Main at Gray, featuring hamburgers and hot dogs for 10 cents each. This is the site where the Trailways Bus Station is today.*

nephew is still serving oysters in the Hyatt Regency garage building.

I was a regular customer at James Coney Island on Walker when a coney island sandwich was still a nickel. I visited the Esperson Drug Store lunch counter a couple of times hoping I could see millionaires making oil deals. It was common talk that the Esperson Drug Store was where they made them, but I never saw any deals being made. There were several drug stores downtown then. They all had lunch counters. The expense account lunch hadn't caught on yet.

The best way to get from Houston to Dallas or Fort Worth then was on the Sam Houston Rocket or the Texas Zephyr. The diesel streamliners were retired in 1966 and 1969, but there is not yet a more civilized way to get to Dallas or Fort Worth.

Memorial Drive was a country lane extending westward from Shepherd. A few people had country homes west of Memorial Park and not many of them guessed what was to

Opposite: *The Kirby Theatre was in the 900 block of Main. The entrance was through the Kirby Building that still stands. Several fashionable stores, including Neiman-Marcus, have occupied the Kirby Building. The upper floors are now office condominiums.*

Above left: *The neighborhood has changed a lot. The new Houston Center is less than a block away. But James Coney Island is still serving lunch on Walker Street between Main and Fannin, where it has been since 1926. The business started in 1923 around the corner on Rusk. There are several branches now and James Papadakis presides over the business. It was established by his father and uncle. His father was Tom Papadakis and his uncle was*

James. *They flipped a coin to decide which name to use.*

Above right: *The Florsheim Company now sells shoes on the site of the old Esperson Drug Store. Oilmen met at the lunch counter here to seal big deals with handshakes, according to local legend. The drug store was in the Mellie Esperson Building at the corner of Travis and Walker.*

Left: *Buster Kern was a homicide detective on the Houston police force before he ran for sheriff in 1948. Kern campaigned on a promise to shut down the brothels and gambling houses in the county. He surprised a lot of people after he was elected by doing what he promised.*

Below: *One of the fine homes on Main Street was the one T.H. Scanlan built for himself and his spinster daughters. The daughters eventually had it dismantled and they used the materials to build another home on their plantation south of town. Scanlan was mayor of Houston during the carpetbag period after the Civil War.*

Opposite: *The home built for laywer R.S. Lovett at 2017 Main stood until the 1940s. There is a McDonald's hamburger stand on the site now. The McDonald chain bought out a local concern of the same name to get the right to use the name McDonald's in Houston.*

become of their wooded wonderland. Many of the fine old homes built in the 1890s and early 1900s still stood on Main Street, but some of them had been converted to rooming houses by the time I got here.

Houston was a wide open town until 1948. Operators of gambling houses and brothels made almost no attempt to hide what they were doing. Jakie Friedman's big white showplace on South Main was especially blatant. Friedman offered dining and dancing, drinking, craps and roulette for the carriage trade. No riffraff and no strangers got past the guardhouse at the entrance to the grounds. Friedman moved on to Las Vegas when Buster Kern was elected sheriff in 1948. Kern put the lid on the town and some former lawmen spent the next several years trying to explain their tax returns to the IRS.

I never got acquainted with Jesse Jones. He didn't have many friends in my set. But I often saw him because he lived on the top floor of the Lamar Hotel where the KPRC studios were. Jones sometimes walked from the hotel to his

Above: *Leon Jaworski is a native Texan and the son of a Baptist preacher. He is a former war crimes prosecutor, former president of the American Bar Association, former Watergate prosecutor and senior partner in one of the biggest law firms in Houston.*

Below: *Oscar Holcombe (in white suit) came to Houston from Alabama and served more years as mayor than anyone else before or since. Holcombe had hay fever. He could not sleep in Houston in the summertime before air conditioning. He tried to spend most of the summer at his retreat outside Hunt. Sometimes he had to be in Houston to tend to city business in the summer. He drove to Galveston every night during those periods and slept on the top floor of the Buccaneer Hotel, where he could breathe.*

office in the Bankers' Mortgage Building. He owned both buildings. He called no attention to himself, but he was not easily mistaken for an ordinary pedestrian. *Imposing* is the word that best fit the late Jesse Jones. He had a black limousine. Sometimes he had his chauffeur drive him to work in that. Sometimes they took the other car. It was a convertible Ford. Jones liked to ride in it with the top down.

The first time I met Leon Jaworski was when he returned from the war crimes trials in Germany to rejoin the law firm then known as Fulbright, Crooker, Freeman, Bates and Jaworski. I had no idea then how many more times I would be interviewing him as he came and went performing significant services for his profession and his country over the ensuing 35 years. Jaworski could have had a position on the U.S. Supreme Court when Lyndon Johnson was president. If he had accepted it, he would not have been available when a special prosecutor was needed in the Watergate case.

Beepers and nervous assignment editors have changed the way reporters work. It was possible before for a broadcast reporter to spend enough time on his stories to get acquainted with some of the principals. News conferences then were less formal, less disputatious and less well attended. Mayor Oscar Holcombe might have had three to five reporters for one of his weekly news conferences before 1950. The reporters all were assigned full time to the city hall and they all knew each other and the mayor well.

There usually were some serious questions and answers, but there was often a lot of conversation too. Holcombe sometimes reminisced about his early political experiences. I remember especially his story about how he handled a crisis in the final week of his second campaign for mayor in 1922. An opponent publicly accused Holcombe of being a gambler and a drunk. Holcombe was neither, but he was a Baptist and he knew the charges would certainly trouble his fellow Baptists. He persuaded his pastor to arrange a public trial with a jury of ministers. The accuser put on his case. Holcombe put on his defense. The ministers decided the mayor was not a gambler or a drunkard. The trial made great publicity and Holcombe was reelected handily. He said he thought all the ministers on the jury voted for him.

An assignment editor might think it a waste for a reporter to spend his time listening to an old man reminiscing about something that happened 30 years earlier. But we didn't have assignment editors then. I never counted as wasted the time I spent during lunch recesses at the courthouse listening to Judge A.C. Winbern's stories about the great murder trials he handled when he was district attorney.

The great murder trials during my days at the courthouse were mostly handled by Percy Foreman. He had been a prosecutor once, briefly, but he was a defense attorney by the time I knew him. And he was the best. Any trial he appeared in during his heyday always drew a full complement of reporters, lawyers and spectators. Foreman tried to act like he didn't notice the attention, but he enjoyed it and sometimes used it to his advantage. He sometimes asked prospective jurors questions like, "You're not going to think my client is guilty just because she hired me, are you?" The prospective jurors usually said, "No." I heard Foreman more than once tell people that he did not claim to be the world's greatest criminal lawyer. He always added that he would not deny it either. Somebody was chiding him once about the size of the fees he charged his clients. Foreman said, "Well, somebody has to punish these criminals."

It was still unusual in 1949 for something happening in Houston to attract national attention, but the opening of the Shamrock Hotel on the night of March 17 of that year attracted plenty. Glenn McCarthy imported 175 Hollywood personalities by special plane and train and he arranged for Dorothy Lamour's NBC network radio show to originate from his new hotel's glittering Emerald Room. A lot of people crashed the party in the Emerald Room. They caused so much noise and commotion that NBC cut the Lamour show off the air. The microphones picked up some language before the show was cut off that had never been heard on a network previously, fairly common Texas expressions, but new to the air. It is generally believed that

Above: *Glenn McCarthy wanted the whole country to take notice when he opened his Shamrock Hotel in 1949. He brought dozens of Hollywood personalities to town for a party that lasted a week. The rooms in the Shamrock were priced from $6 a night up when the hotel opened.*

Right: *Percy Foreman grew up in Lufkin, where his father was sheriff. Watching trials convinced him he should be a lawyer. He became one of the most famous defense lawyers in the country after he moved to Houston. He kept his small town manners. They are often useful in dealing with juries. But Foreman can also be as suave as anybody when he wants to.*

Edna Ferber found part of the inspiration for her novel *Giant* in the Shamrock opening.

Television came to Houston on January 1, 1949, when hotel man Albert Lee put KLEE-TV, Channel 2, on the air. The identification announcement he used was "KLEE-TV, Channel 2 in Houston, the Eyes of Texas." I borrowed his slogan 20 years later when I needed a title for a television magazine program about Texas. Lee did not do well with his television station; so he was ready to sell it a couple of years later. The Houston Post Company bought it. The Post already owned KPRC Radio and the name of the television station was changed to KPRC-TV. It was the only TV station in Houston for several years. Channel 11 started in Galveston as KGUL-TV, moved to Houston in 1958 and changed its name to KHOU. It was owned originally by local people, but is now part of the Corinthian chain, owned by Dun and Bradstreet. KTRK-TV, Channel 13, went on the air in 1954. It was owned originally by a syndicate of wealthy Houstonians. They sold it in 1967 to the Capital Cities

Opposite left: *The first television station in Houston operated in this Quonset hut on the grounds of Pin Oak Stables on South Post Oak Road. An office complex is being developed on the property and the old TV station will soon be gone.*

Opposite right: *The original television station was Channel 2. It is housed now in this* building on the Southwest Freeway in Sharpstown. Channel 2 is the NBC affiliate in Houston.

Top: *The CBS station in Houston is Channel 11 on Allen Parkway near downtown.*

Bottom: *The ABC station is on Bissonnet off Buffalo Speedway. This is Channel 13.*

chain. Albert Lee was the only person ever to lose money in VHF television in Houston.

The first television newsman in Houston was Tom Journay. He worked for Channel 2 when it was KLEE-TV. Marvin Zindler worked for KLEE—TV occasionally as a reporter. Pat Flaherty was news director for KPRC Radio. He became news director for both stations when the Post bought the TV station. The KPRC Radio news staff provided news for the television station. We did it in the beginning as a sideline. The radio station was the big end of the business, but television news got more of the news department's attention as the television audience grew. We got our own film camera in 1953. It was a Bell and Howell Carrera. Reporter Bob Gray got the responsibility for carrying the camera and making our news film. Bob is now president of Cordovan Publishing Company. He taught me how to make motion pictures and edit film. I was the first substitute news cameraman in Houston television. All our news film before this had been furnished by contractors. Bob and I worked as a team in the early days, covering the court-house, the city hall and police station and going to fires and murder scenes. Bob usually handled the camera and I was the reporter, but sometimes we switched roles. This was the period of my career I enjoyed the most. If I have any regret, it is that I later spent so many years fiddling with administrative details and trying to manage people who mostly did not wish to be managed. A writer ought to write.

Television was largely responsible for the first Salt Grass Trail Ride. The idea came out of a conversation between

Above: *The earliest picture of the author on television is this shot a viewer snapped off her TV screen. Foley's had just one store, downtown, at the time. The company was one of the earliest and most enthusiastic television news sponsors.*

Right: *The first full-time television news cameraman in Houston was Bob Gray.*

Opposite: *The best known television performer in Houston is Channel 13's consumer crusader, Marvin Zindler. He was one of the first television news reporters here. He is most famous for embarrassing Governor Dolph Briscoe into ordering the closing of the bawdy house that has since become known as "The Best Little Whorehouse in Texas."*

Top: *The Salt Grass Trail Ride to the Houston Fat Stock Show began in 1952. The city's original television news director was one of the four men to make the ride the first year. Pat Flaherty was a regular on the trail every year from 1952 until he died. He is on the right in this picture.*

Bottom: *The idea of roughing it for a few days on horseback or in a wagon proved contagious. Thousands of people took it up. They follow several different trails into Houston for the stock show every year. They don't mind that the show opens at the end of February when the weather is often disagreeable, as it was when the riders arrived downtown in 1982.*

Channel 2 manager Jack Harris and advertising agent Charlie Geizendanner. Charlie was responsible for publicity for the annual Houston Fat Stock Show. He was looking for ways to get more people interested in the show. Either he or Jack hit upon the idea of getting someone to ride into Houston in a covered wagon from some outlying town for the next stock show. Jack volunteered to have Pat Flaherty make the trip. Pat was news director for the only television station in town, so there was sure to be news coverage. I think Jack may have thought he was imposing upon Flaherty, but Jack is never reluctant to impose. It is his style.

Three other men made that first ride with Flaherty. Emil Marks and John Warnash both were old-time cowmen. Reese Lockett was the mayor of Brenham and a veteran rodeo producer. Flaherty made frequent reports on their progress. Their ride from Brenham to Houston for the 1952 stock show generated more publicity than anything connected with the show ever had before. Dozens of people wanted to know if they could make the next trip. An association was formed. It has been growing ever since and many similar groups have been formed to ride in from other points. That trail ride surely was one of the most successful promotions in the history of promotion. And it never was an imposition. Pat Flaherty had the time of his life on that first ride and the Salt Grass Trail Ride was the high point of his year for the few years he had left to live. His obvious enjoyment encouraged thousands of others to try playing cowboy.

The early 1950s brought a great boom in home building in Houston and nearly everywhere else. The Miller family got a VA loan and a bungalow in one of the new suburbs beyond the city limits. Most of the home building took place outside the city limits for the same reason much of it still does. The land is cheaper. Buyers are attracted because they don't have to pay city taxes until the city annexes them. It didn't take long for that to happen to our subdivision.

But there were greater worries than city taxes for the

Center: *Felix Tijerina was born in Texas, but he knew no English when he started working as a restaurant busboy. Felix spent a lot of time and energy after he became successful trying to help young Mexican-Americans learn some English words before they entered the public schools. Houston School Superintendent Billy Reagan taught in one of Tijerina's schools when he was a young man.*

Top: *The Houston Independent School District has honored the late Tijerina for his contributions to education by naming a new elementary school for him. The school is on Sherman Street on the east side, where much of the city's Latin population is concentrated.*

Bottom: *Barbara Jordan was often on the podium at black rallies and protest meetings in the 1960s. She was elected to the Texas Senate in 1966 and to the U.S. Congress in 1972. She retired in 1978 and is now teaching at the Lyndon Johnson School of Public Affairs at the University of Texas at Austin.*

parents of young children in the 1950s. Polio crippled many young people every summer. The worst year in Houston was 1953. There were 125 paralytic cases in Houston that year. No one was sure what the cause was. Overexertion and heat were thought to have something to do with it; so mothers tried to keep their children indoors during the hottest part of the day. The Salk vaccine was perfected in 1955. That was the most welcome news I ever reported.

People sometimes say that news reporters never tell the good things people do. Maybe we don't tell enough, but I remember thinking it was a good thing when I reported on Felix Tijerina and his "Little Schools of Four Hundred." Felix started out as a busboy in a Houston restaurant and learned English from the menus. He went on to open his own restaurant and build the Felix Mexican Restaurant chain. He used part of the money he made to sponsor schools where Mexican children learned the 400 basic English words Felix knew they had to know in order to learn anything in public schools. It never occurred to Felix that the public schools should teach Mexican children in their own language.

I don't remember what night it was. I am not even sure of the year. But cameraman Charles Farris and I went to a church in the Third Ward one night in the early 1960s to cover a protest meeting. I think the reason for the protest was a school bond issue the blacks figured was intended to reinforce segregation. I could be wrong about the reason. What stands out about the event in my memory is that Barbara Jordan spoke. It was the first time I ever heard that voice. It was also the first time I ever heard "We Shall Overcome." I left that church convinced that they surely would.

The air in Houston and the water in Buffalo Bayou were polluted long before my time. The Environmental Protection Agency is still fussing about the ozone level and the bayou is still a mess, but there has been some improvement since the 1960s. The legislature created the Texas Water Pollution Control Board in 1961 and the Texas Air Control Board in 1965 and the Gulf Coast Waste Disposal Authority was formed in 1970. These agencies were created to some extent because of Dr. Walter Quebedeaux. He was almost a folk hero.

The Harris County Commissioners' Court hired Walter Quebedeaux in 1953 to direct the county's pollution control service. I do not know how serious the commissioners were about controlling pollution. They got Quebedeaux from the Champion Paper mill. That mill was the source of some of the worst pollution at the time, but Quebedeaux took his appointment seriously. He jumped on Champion and other polluters without favor. He filed suits against 50 companies during his first two years in office and forced most of them to install new pollution control equipment. He made personal inspections unannounced and he clashed with plant security people more than once. And he told the awful truth about the cities of Houston and Pasadena. The cities had never come down hard on polluters because they were among the worst offenders with their incinerators and overloaded sewage treatment plants. Rumors often surfaced that the commissioners planned to fire Dr. Quebedeaux or wanted to fire him, but they never did. He had too many fans. He remained in office until he died of a heart attack in 1976 at the age of 61.

I met George Bush shortly after he moved to Houston from Midland in 1958. This required no effort on my part. George was deliberately meeting people in the news business as part of his plan to run for public office. He told people he had made enough money in the oil business so that he didn't have to work any more and he meant to spend the rest of his years in public service. He made a respectable showing in his race for the U.S. Senate in 1964 and was elected to the U.S. House of Representatives in 1966. Cameraman Gary James and I went to Washington to file TV reports on his and Congressman Bob Eckhardt's first few days in office.

I was swimming with Congressman Bush off Miami Beach the afternoon after the Republicans nominated Richard Nixon for president. That was 1968. Nixon and his advisers were meeting while we swam. They were deciding

Above: A bronze tablet on the lawn outside the Family Law Center in the County Courthouse Complex on Congress Avenue is a tribute to the late Dr. Walter Quebedeaux. He won a big personal following with his tough stance against polluters as Harris County's original director of pollution control.

Right: Vice President George Bush is a patrician for the Eastern shore and he has a degree from Yale. But when he says he is a Texan, Texans don't dispute it. He moved to Midland when he was fresh out of college. He got a job in the oil business and he helped found the company that became Zapata Offshore before he started his political career in Houston in the 1960s.

on a candidate for vice president. George Bush was one of the people mentioned in the speculation. George insisted that he didn't think he had a chance, but it was plain the nomination for vice president was something he would very much like to have. No one knows how much turmoil we might have been spared if Nixon had chosen Bush that day instead of Spiro Agnew.

The Astrodome opened the evening of April 9, 1965. The Houston Astros beat the New York Yankees in the first game under the plastic roof. I did not cover the game. I know my limitations — some of them anyway. I did do a live report for the early news on the opening ceremonies. President and Mrs. Lyndon Johnson were there along with Governor John Connally and his wife, Nellie. It must have been the high point of Judge Roy Hofheinz's career. Hofheinz had had many high points. He had been county judge and mayor of Houston before he got interested in promoting the stadium. He concentrated most of his phenomenal energy and attention on the dome project for four years. He knew every detail and dimension. The Radio and Television News Directors' Association held a convention here in 1964. Ray Conaway of KTRK-TV and I were the hosts. We arranged a buffet dinner at the Astrodome and asked Hofheinz to tell the news directors about some of the features to be included in the stadium. It was unfinished, but the frame was up. We sat in temporary seats while the judge talked and talked. He explained in the greatest detail the problems that had been anticipated and solved during the planning. There were many of them, but the news directors remembered one better than the others. News directors from elsewhere were still asking Conaway and me years later whether it came to pass that all the toilets in the dome really could be flushed at the same time. It was one of the promises Hofheinz made. He delivered on it as far as I know.

I got to watch Dr. Michael DeBakey install an artificial heart valve in a patient at Methodist Hospital when that was one of the more daring operations heart surgeons were doing. It was well before DeBakey and Dr. Denton Cooley

The landmark that symbolizes Houston more than any other was completed and opened in 1965. President Lyndon Johnson and Governor John Connally attended the ceremony opening the covered stadium Roy Hofheinz had decided to call the Astrodome. Harris County owns the Astrodome and the county insists upon calling it the Harris County Domed Stadium. Roy Hofheinz no longer has any connection with the sports association that holds the lease, but the name he chose is the name that stuck. This is not inappropriate. Hofheinz contributed several times as much time, energy and imagination as any other individual to the campaign that produced the stadium and won the National League baseball franchise for Houston. Hofheinz had to change some of his original ideas. Sunlight coming through the plastic roof blinded the outfielders and the roof had to be darkened with paint. The lack of daylight killed the grass and Hofheinz substituted an artificial grass developed by Monsanto. The man behind Mrs. Johnson in this photograph is Welcome Wilson. The man behind the president is Johnny Goyen.

began transplanting hearts and experimenting with artificial hearts.

We made a live news special out of the parade welcoming the original seven astronauts to Houston on the 4th of July in 1962. They were transferred here from Virginia when the National Aeronautics and Space Administration began building the Manned Spacecraft Center at Clear Lake. They were celebrities of the first rank, especially John Glenn. He had just completed the first orbital flight. The astronauts' arrival validated Houston's "Space City" claims and did more for real estate values around Clear Lake than anything ever had. Tom Wolfe makes it appear in his book *The Right Stuff* that Houston officials broiled the astronauts and their families in open cars, then chilled them in the air-conditioned Sam Houston Coliseum and there forced on them several hospitable gestures Wolfe considered clumsy and crude. If the astronauts shared Wolfe's opinion of the welcome, they didn't let on. I thought they were having a good time.

We reporters spent a lot of time in the 1960s camped outside the various astronauts' houses while they were making the Gemini and Apollo flights. There was always the remote chance that a wife or child might do or say something interesting while the astronaut was in orbit. The families all knew we were there also in case something unthinkable happened to the spaceship.

I was at the Manned Spacecraft Center in 1969 on the day Neil Armstrong put that first footprint on the moon. I have not seen that many people that happy about anything

Top right: *Armstrong's radio announcement that he had landed at what NASA had decided to call Tranquility Base touched off a joyous celebration in the Mission Control Center at the space base. The man at the far right is Dr. Robert Gilruth, director of the Manned Spacecraft Center at the time. The third man from the right is Dr. Christopher Kraft. He was flight director then and he later succeeded Gilruth as head of the center. Kraft was with the manned space flight program from the start. He complained when he retired in 1982 that the Reagan administration was doing too little to maintain the American lead in space.*

Bottom right: *The television networks sent their top newsmen to cover the space flights in the 1960s. Chet Huntley and David Brinkley used to do their reports from a glass studio on top of the Nassau Bay Motor Inn across Nasa Road I from the space center. The studio has been demolished. Walter Cronkite used an indoor studio a few doors to the east.*

Opposite: *Houstonians put out the red carpet on the Fourth of July, 1962, to welcome the first astronauts. The National Aeronautics and Space Administration transferred the astronauts here when the agency started building the space center at Clear Lake. Real estate developer Frank Sharp offered to give each of the seven astronauts a $60,000 home in his new Sharpstown subdivision. The space agency said no. But the astronauts managed to make pretty good deals on new homes closer to the space base.*

since. Some reporter asked one of the NASA people what time it was on the moon and the official gloated, "The moon is on Houston time."

President John Kennedy spent part of the last evening of his life in the Sam Houston Coliseum. The occasion was a dinner honoring veteran Congressman Albert Thomas. It was part of a tour the president was making to gather support for his reelection bid. The president made a speech about people perishing where there is no vision. He said Albert Thomas had the kind of vision that keeps people from perishing. President and Mrs. Kennedy flew to Fort Worth after the dinner here. They spent the night in Fort Worth and flew to Dallas the next morning.

I remember talking with Jack Valenti about some of the details of the Thomas dinner a few hours before it started. I was planning our TV coverage. Jack was in charge of the arrangements. He had an advertising business in Houston then and was a volunteer aide to Thomas and to Vice President Lyndon Johnson. The vice president invited Valenti to join his party for the rest of the Texas tour after the Thomas dinner. That is how it happened that Valenti was aboard Johnson's plane when Johnson was sworn in as president at the Dallas airport. The Houston ad man was in Washington working for the new president of the United States by that night, 24 hours after he had left the Coliseum.

Jack had helped us arrange a television visit to the LBJ Ranch at Stonewall a few months earlier. It was before portable TV cameras were developed. We took two truckloads of big studio cameras and tape recorders to the ranch and spent two days making pictures and recording interviews with the vice president and his wife and daughters. Director Bob Marich edited the tape into an hour program, but it was never aired. It no longer seemed appropriate after President Kennedy was killed and Johnson became president. NBC did use on the night of the assassination some of the comments Johnson made to us about his philosophy and his aims. They were about the only current Johnson comments available. No one else had paid much

Texas Democrats were fighting among themselves in 1963. President John Kennedy wanted them to put aside their differences long enough to help him get reelected in 1964. So the president and Vice President Lyndon Johnson came to Texas November 21, 1963, to promote harmony. They visited San Antonio that afternoon and came to Houston that evening for a dinner honoring Congressman Albert Thomas. Democrats of all factions were on hand to hear the president praise Thomas's vision. The president and the vice president thought things were going well as they flew on to Fort Worth that night and to Dallas the next morning.

31

attention to Johnson while he was vice president.

President Richard Nixon came to Houston in March of 1974 when he was trying to rise above the Watergate scandal. Some of his aides had been indicted by then. The special prosecutor and the House committee were demanding additional tapes and documents Nixon did not want to furnish. He was on a campaign to generate public support for his claim that the doctrine of Executive Privilege entitled him to refuse the demands. The president had received a warm reception at a meeting of business executives in Chicago a few days earlier. He came to Houston to appear before a group he expected to be every bit as friendly. The National Association of Broadcasters was in convention here. The members are the owners and managers of radio and television stations. They all hold licenses from the government. No one is less anxious to offend a sitting president. Nixon and his staff probably expected that the owners and managers would ask the questions at the news conference the president volunteered to hold. But the owners and managers passed the responsibility for making the arrangements and asking the questions to the Radio and Television News Directors' Association.

Bos Johnson of West Virginia was president of the news directors' organization and he asked me to help him with the arrangements. The event was staged in Jones Hall. Members of the National Association of Broadcasters and a good many local Nixon backers were in the audience. About 100 broadcast newsmen from southwest stations were on the stage. Some of them happened also to be owners or managers of their stations. The regular network correspondents assigned to the White House were on the stage too. Presidential press secretary Ron Ziegler made it plain to us that he hoped White House correspondents would not be allowed any part in the proceedings. He said the president wanted local people to be able to ask him questions. We made no promises. Usually at a regular presidential news conference, the president decides which reporter will ask the next question. I was designated to

President Richard Nixon came to Houston in the spring of 1974 when he was trying to offset the damage the Watergate scandal had done. It was in Jones Hall on the night of March 19, 1974, that the president and CBS correspondent Dan Rather confronted each other in the incident some people remember better than anything else about the Watergate period. Nixon supporters will always believe that Rather "sassed" the president.

make the decisions that night.

The whole show was on television live. The early questions were mild and general and the president got to make most of the comments he came to make. Finally somebody did ask a Watergate question and the president made an answer that indicated he was cooperating fully with the investigation. The network correspondents all wanted to jump in then. All three were friends of mine. I had known Dan Rather of CBS since we both were radio reporters, before his reporting of Hurricane Carla attracted the network's attention. Tom Brokaw was there for the network my station was affiliated with. Tom Jarriel of ABC was a former Channel 2 colleague and a cherished friend. It seemed to me by this time that we were being used to a degree that was going to be a lasting embarrassment. I picked Dan Rather to ask the next question.

Nixon was still elaborating on his answer to the previous question when Rather took his position at the microphone. The president did not appear to be pleased. It seemed to me that he drew out his response to the previous question more than necessary. Finally he stopped. He had been very gracious with the previous questioners, nodding or saying something to invite them to introduce themselves. He just stared at Rather. There was a short silence. Rather saw that he would have to speak first and spoke the standard correspondent's line, "Mr. President, Dan Rather, CBS News." The audience had been applauding all of Nixon's sallies up to this point. There was a little applause when Dan introduced himself, but the applause was drown-

Opposite top: *Dan Rather is a native Texan. He grew up in Houston and he was news director for Channel 11 here in 1961. His reporting of Hurricane Carla that fall impressed the brass at CBS and the network hired him.*

Opposite bottom: *The correspondent representing ABC during the 1974 Nixon visit was* *another former Houston newsman. Tom Jarriel was working for Channel 2 during Hurricane Carla. His coverage of that storm helped him move up to the network job.*

ed out by the boos. Some Nixon boosters perceived Rather an enemy. The president listened to the applause and the boos for a few seconds and asked, "Are you running for something?" Dan says he was uncertain whether the president was being sarcastic or joking; so he made a reply that seemed appropriate in either case. But I suspect that his reply and the president's question were both spontaneous. Rather answered, "No sir, Mr. President, are you?" There was more booing from the Nixon partisans in the audience, but Rather went on with his question. He asked how the House of Representatives could carry out its duties in the impeachment process if the president continued to withhold evidence the House wanted. The president said the House was trying to go beyond the constitutional grounds for impeachment.

Jarriel and Brokow both got in questions on Watergate too. But nothing got as much attention as Nixon's and Rather's opening remarks to each other. NBC News President Reuven Frank has been quoted since as saying that Rather "smart-assed" the president. CBS News President Dick Salant told me the managers of several CBS stations were after him to do something about his upstart White House correspondent. I caught a lot of flack for letting big time network correspondents steal the show from the local folks, but I never regretted what I did. It produced the only interesting thing that happened that night.

I remember meeting Gerald Hines when he was building some tasteful but modest office buildings along Richmond Avenue, gathering the momentum for the Galleria project that would propel him into the front rank among developers. He was the same precise and unpretentious personality then. He and Kenneth Schnitzer have had more to do than anyone else with bringing style to the Houston skyline.

Kenneth Schnitzer started developing Greenway Plaza in the 1960s on some vacant land he bought at Richmond Avenue and Buffalo Speedway, just off the Southwest Freeway. He anticipated that he would want to expand the development beyond the original dimensions; so he began buying up the houses in the adjoining Lamar Weslayan

Above: *Gerald D. Hines probably has put up more buildings than any other single developer in the country. Hines was born in Indiana. He came to Houston in 1948. His first project was the renovation of an office building in 1951. His first big project was the Galleria shopping complex. He has since built major buildings and shopping centers all over the world. His trademark is striking design.*

Below: *Developer Kenneth Schnitzer has concentrated most of his attention on his Greenway Plaza development, where he has created a blend of commercial and residential buildings with entertainment centers and imaginative landscaping. Schnitzer is now working on some major buildings downtown, too.*

subdivision. He made the owners fairly generous offers and he allowed them to continue living in their houses until he actually needed the land. He had bought most of the property on the three short streets in the subdivision by 1969. The few people still holding onto their property wanted more money. Schnitzer came to terms one at a time with all the owners except Jim and Dorothy Lee. They had a three-bedroom brick bungalow on Norfolk Street that would have been worth at the time about $26,000 if it had

Above and right: *Houston was developing a style of architecture in keeping with the Sadie Thompson climate before air conditioning encouraged the architects to ignore the climate. The old Rice Hotel, the original Texaco building and many other early buildings had generous and very useful canopies over the sidewalks.*

Opposite: *Jim and Dorothy Lee did what many Houstonians dream of doing. They sold Kenneth Schnitzer a house for more than 20 times what they paid for it. The house was on land Schnitzer needed for Greenway Plaza. It is this kind of happening that keeps Houstonians from wanting zoning. The condominium tower behind the Lees here is standing on what was their back yard.*

40

been somewhere else.

Dorothy came from Australia. Jim was born in Houston. They said they were happy on Norfolk Street. They did not want to move, but they would 'move for half a million dollars. Schnitzer pretended for a time that the price was out of the question, but he had to have the Lee property. He paid them their price in 1974.

The Lees used part of the money to buy a bigger house on a golf course in the next county. Living well somewhere else on some developer's money may be the native Houstonian's best revenge. ■

The current trend in architecture is toward vast open plazas around the new office buildings. They are handsome, but a pedestrian could drown trying to get from the curb to the doorway here during one of our monsoons. Most of the new office buildings downtown, though, are served by a system of underground tunnels. Many office workers can use these tunnels to travel between their parking garages and their offices and avoid the weather completely. But it is well to remember that the underground garages depend upon pumps to keep them from flooding during the heavy rains. The pumps can fail. Houstonians are careful where they park during the floods and NEVER buy a used car right after a flood. Maps of the tunnel system may be obtained from the public library, the downtown banks or from the security guards in the tunnels.

Houston is crapemyrtles in the summer sun. The lush vegetation here surprises many visitors. The oaks, the pines, the cypresses and the magnolias are natives. The crapemyrtles were imported. They probably grew first in China. They were growing in Europe by 1600 and in Virginia by 1800. The first cuttings were brought to Houston more than 100 years ago. Crapemyrtles resist most insects and diseases. They like the climate in Houston and bloom most of the summer. Landscape architects are partial to them, so they grace some of the fanciest neighborhoods. They are easy to start from cuttings and they require little care, so they flourish in the humblest neighborhoods as well. The colors are red, purple, white and several shades of pink.

Houston is spectacular architecture. Many of the city's buildings were designed by the top architects in the country. There is an increasing trend toward fountains and displays of modern sculpture in the plazas around the commercial buildings. Houstonians have mixed feelings toward some of these, like the Joan Miro figure outside the new Texas Commerce Tower, designed by I.M. Pei.

Houston is a cultural melange. The range is from ballet and symphonic concerts at the elegant Jones Hall to the Cotton-eyed Joe and kicker concerts at the country and western clubs, with plenty of ethnic diversions in between. Gilley's in Pasadena has become a major tourist attraction. Cross-country drivers jam the parking lot with their big rigs. Grandmothers bring their grandchildren in strollers and stand in line to pay the $6.00 cover charge.

47

Houston is growth and progress. The growth during the past ten years has been more than the freeway system was designed to accommodate. The West Loop is now the most congested thoroughfare in the state. Helicopters are the preferred conveyances among Houstonians able to afford them. Houston is home base for one of the Goodyear blimps and the space shuttle sometimes stops here on its trips from the landing site in California to the launching site in Florida.

Houston is unlimited educational opportunities. Students and staffers from the world famous Medical Center play soccer on the neighboring campus of Rice University. The University of Houston is piling up its own imposing skyline in the shadow of the downtown skyline, and the brooding statue of William Marsh Rice dominates the quadrangle on the campus of the university he made possible.

Houston is big-time sports in the renowned Astrodome. The bubble-top stadium is the home of the Houston Oilers and the Houston Astros. The Houston Rockets play their basketball games in the Summit Arena.

Houston is cowboys of all degrees. The city never was a real cowtown. No cattle trails came this way. But aggressive promotion has made the Houston Livestock Show and Rodeo the biggest event of its kind in the world. So the top professional cowboys in the country come here to compete for the big prizes every spring. And the urban cowboys tangle with the mechanical bulls at Gilley's every night.

Houston is capital of the world of oil. Many of the leading experts in the discovery and production of oil and gas and most of the industry trouble shooters make their homes here. No other area anywhere has as many refineries and petrochemical plants as the Houston Ship Channel.

Identification of color photographs on the preceeding pages.

P 43   *Crapemyrtles on Memorial Drive.*
P 44   Above: *The fountains in Tranquility Park.*
        Below left: *Joan Miro sculpture, Texas Commerce Tower.*
        Below right: *The downtown skyline from I-45 North.*
P 45   *Looking south on Milam Street from near the McKinney intersection.*
P 46   Above: *Fireworks over Astroworld Park.*
        Center left: *The growing Chinese neighborhood on the near east side of town.*
        Center right: *The Jesse H. Jones Hall for the Performing Arts.*
P 47   Center left: *Las Cazuelas Restaurant on Fulton.*
        Center right: *The Athens Restaurant, also known as the Athens Bar and Grill.*
        Below left and right: *Gilley's country and western nightclub in Pasadena.*
P 48   Center: *Traffic on the West Loop between Memorial and the Southwest Freeway.*
        Below left: *The Houston skyline during the 1982 lunar eclipse.*
        Below right: *NASA transport plane and the Space Shuttle landing at Ellington Air Force Base.*
P 49   *Two Goodyear blimps survey the city.*
P 50   Above: *Soccer teams from the schools in the Texas Medical Center clash on the campus of Rice University.*
        Below: *University of Houston main campus.*
P 51   *The Quadrangle and William Marsh Rice statue, Rice University campus.*
P 52   Center: *The Astrodome during a night game.*
        Below: *Earl Campbell.*
P 53   Above: *The Astros playing to a nearly full house.*
        Below: *Joe Sambito.*
P 54   *Bullrider, 1982 Houston Fat Stock Show and Rodeo.*
P 55   *Bullrider, Gilley's.*
P 56   Center left: *Red Adair's wild well crew sprays a burning offshore gas well.*
        Center: *The old Goose Creek Oil Field near Baytown.*
        Below: *The Exxon Refinery at Baytown.*
P 57   *Most of the docks on the ship channel are within sight of the Houston skyline.*
P 58   *Infrared photograph of Houston area taken from an RB-57 aircraft flying at 60,000 ft., NASA Earth Resources Aircraft Program Mission 438, March 1981.*

PART TWO

Early History 1836-1899

"The town of Houston is located at a point on the river which must ever command the trade of the largest and richest portion of Texas. . ." Excerpt from the founders' original advertisement.

Architect Philip Johnson has said that Houston is the last great 19th century city where people are not afraid to try anything. Douglas Milburn called it the "Last American City" in the book he wrote about it. Whether it is either or neither of these, Houston started as a scheme to make money. John Kirby Allen and his brother Augustus were looking for land they could sell for more than they had to pay for it when they came up Buffalo Bayou in the summer of 1836. The imprint of that beginning is likely to be part of Houston's character forever. But an imprint is not necessarily a stigma.

Texas had been Spanish territory for 300 years when Moses Austin in 1821 persuaded the Spanish to let him bring in some Anglo settlers from the United States. Moses Austin died and Spain lost control of the territory shortly after that, but Moses's son negotiated a new deal with the new Mexican government. Buffalo Bayou was on the eastern edge of the colony Stephen F. Austin developed. The land where Houston is today was granted to John Austin.

Relations between Mexican authorities and the Anglo colonists never became really cordial. Mexican colonial policies and attitudes changed several times as the Mexican government changed. Some of the colonists resented the way they were treated. Some of the Mexican settlers resented the presence of outsiders. The Mexican government was trying to limit further Anglo immigration by the early 1830s. Some of the Anglo colonists were agitating for a separate state government.

Houstonians almost never refer to their town as "The Bayou City." This is a term used by writers but by hardly anybody else. A bayou is a short stream on the Gulf Coast that would be called a creek if it were somewhere else. A bayou in Louisiana usually is called a BY-YOU. A bayou in Texas usually is called a BY-OH. But you may hear the word pronounced either way in either place. Some historians claim Buffalo Bayou was named for the buffalo fish, but it probably was named for the buffalo. Some very early maps had it labelled Buffalo River. It is not big enough to be a river. But Buffalo Bayou has been Houston's biggest asset from the beginning.

JOHN KIRBY
ALLEN

BORN IN CANASAREAUGH, NEW YORK
1810 · CAME TO TEXAS IN 1832 ·
DIED IN HOUSTON AUGUST 18, 1838

Erected by the State of Texas
1936

Texas had agents in the United States by 1835 enlisting volunteers to fight against Mexico. Volunteers without any legal status were coming in, looking for action. They were the original illegal aliens in Texas. Davy Crockett and some others went to San Antonio and joined the little garrison in the Alamo after Texans seized it from the Mexicans in December, 1835. Mexican authorities realized that they were losing control, so Mexican President Antonio Lopez de Santa Anna gathered up an army and headed for Texas. He was determined to put down the rebellion and more. He planned to chase all the Anglos out of Texas.

Santa Anna was in San Antonio preparing to attack the Alamo when 59 people met at Washington-on-the-Brazos to sign a document declaring Texas free and independent. They all said they were Texans, but only two of the people there on March 2, 1836, had been born in Texas. Several others were bona fide settlers. Some had been in Texas as long as 10 years, but several others had been in Texas less than a year. Sixteen of the signers had come from Tennessee.

Top left: *John Kirby Allen died before the town he and his brother founded was two years old. John was just 29 years old when he died.*

Top right: *Augustus C. Allen was John Allen's older brother. The brothers came to Texas in 1832. They established the town of Houston shortly after the Battle of San Jacinto in 1836. Augustus Allen withdrew from the Allen enterprises in 1850 and left Houston. He died in Washington in 1864. He is buried in Brooklyn.*

Center: *John Allen is buried in Founder's Cemetery on West Dallas near downtown Houston. This cemetery was beyond the city limits on the road to San Felipe when it was established.*

Bottom left: *The Allens were New Yorkers. The whole family came to Texas after John and Augustus founded the town. Their mother and father and four older brothers were living here by the time John died.*

Bottom right: *The land the Allen brothers chose for their townsite had been part of the Stephen F. Austin colony before the revolution. Austin's was the first Anglo colony in Texas sanctioned by the Mexican government.*

Sam Houston and several of the other signers from Tennessee had been friends and political allies of President Andrew Jackson there. Everybody knew Jackson wanted to expand the United States to the west. Many people believe the separation of Texas from Mexico was a Washington idea.

Santa Anna's Mexicans overwhelmed the Alamo garrison on March 6 and started eastward. They looted and burned homes and villages to terrorize the settlers. The settlers fled with what possessions they could carry. Sam Houston and his Texas Army also maneuvered to stay out of the way of the advancing Mexican columns. Santa Anna had things going his way. He heard that the interim government of Texas was at Harrisburg on Buffalo Bayou. He headed for Harrisburg to try to capture the rebel leaders. The Texas officials got away from Harrisburg just in time. The Mexicans burned Harrisburg and, on April 16, they looted the homes along the bayou and around Morgan's Point.

Top right: *Mexican President Antonio Lopez de Santa Anna came to Texas in the spring of 1836 to chase the Anglo colonists out. He had decided they never were going to make satisfactory Mexican citizens. Santa Anna captured the Alamo, but he was surprised, defeated and taken prisoner at San Jacinto on the outskirts of the present city of Houston.*

Top left: *Santa Anna was not concentrating on the war when the Texas Army swarmed into his camp the afternoon of April 21, 1836. The president was closeted with a new girlfriend in his tent about where this marker now stands.*

Bottom: *Sam Houston commanded the Texas forces at San Jacinto. His troops wanted him to kill Santa Anna because the Mexican president had slaughtered the garrison at the Alamo and executed the Texans captured in another battle near Goliad. But Houston considered it better strategy to keep the Mexican leader as a hostage until all the Mexican troops left Texas. Sam Houston was wounded at San Jacinto, but he recovered in time to be elected president of the Republic of Texas in the fall of 1836.*

Sam Houston and the Texas Army showed up in the same vicinity. The Texans and Mexicans selected camp sites within sight of each other on the plain that has been called the San Jacinto Battleground ever since. Santa Anna was satisfied the war was over. He had the rebel government and all the settlers on the run. He had the enemy army in a position where he could attack any time he wanted. He apparently thought he deserved a little break. The Mexican president was relaxing in his fancy campaign tent with a young woman named Emily Morgan at midafternoon on April 21 when Sam Houston and the Texas Army stormed into his camp and put an end to the war and the Mexican rule over Texas. Emily Morgan was a mulatto servant in Col. James Morgan's house at Morgan's Point. Santa Anna's troops had taken her prisoner a few days before the battle. She never got any official credit for her role at San Jacinto, but she is still remembered in the folk song she inspired, "The Yellow Rose of Texas."

The principal settlements in what is now Harris County before the Battle of San Jacinto were Harrisburg, Lynchburg, New Washington and New Kentucky. Harrisburg, Lynchburg and New Washington all were on Buffalo Bayou. New Kentucky was inland near the present town of Tomball. Harrisburg was an important port. Supplies for the Austin colony came to Harrisburg by ship and then were hauled by ox cart to San Felipe and other inland settlements. Houston did not exist.

John and Augustus Allen were New Yorkers. They had come to Texas in 1832 to speculate in land and land claims. They managed to avoid military duty when the fighting started, but they did donate a ship to the Texas Navy. The Allens apparently were the first to realize what an opportunity Santa Anna had created when he burned Harrisburg. The new republic needed a port. The Allens made an offer for what was left of Harrisburg, but there were problems with the title. So they rented a boat and sailed up Buffalo Bayou looking for another likely site. They were taken with the land around the junction of White Oak Bayou and Buffalo Bayou. It was the John Austin grant.

Austin had died. The Allens gave Austin's widow $1,000 cash and a note for $4,000 in exchange for 2,000 acres on the west bank of the bayou. They called in Gail Borden to lay out a townsite. Borden is the man Houstonians can thank for the wide streets downtown. The Allens named several of the streets for heroes of the revolution. They named their town for the hero of San Jacinto because by this time they had decided their new port should also be the capital of the new republic.

The Allen brothers named their new town for Sam Houston as part of their campaign to get the government of the republic to make the town its headquarters. A Congress Square was provided in the original plan of Houston, executed by Gail Borden. Congress Square later became Market Square. Gail Borden later founded the Borden Milk Company.

There were some other contenders for the capital, but the Allens had some advantages. The man they named their town for was elected president of the republic almost immediately afterward and John Allen was elected a member of Congress. He was also appointed a member of President Houston's staff. He and his brother persuaded the president and the Congress that the new government should make its headquarters in the town named for Sam Houston. The decision was made during the first session of

The government of the Republic of Texas moved to Houston in 1837 and conducted its business until 1839 in a building owned by the Allen brothers. The Allens charged no rent. They regained control of the capitol building when the government moved to Austin. The building then was used as a hotel.

the Texas Congress at Columbia in the spring of 1837.

The Allens may have passed out a little free land to make sure the decision came out right. Sam Houston wound up with 12 lots in the new city. The deed records indicate that Houston paid for the lots. Houston told people they were given to him. He gave several of them away. He gave one to a sailor he had never seen before. The occasion was a public ceremony in Houston marking the first anniversary of the Battle of San Jacinto. Marquis James says in his book *The Raven* that the Lone Star flag got tangled in its halyard so that it was not waving properly from the flagpole. The sailor from the visiting schooner *Rolla* climbed the pole and straightened out the flag. The president called him over when he got back down and gave him a lot.

Houston was never a frontier town. There were substantial settlements much farther west long before Houston was established. But it certainly was a primitive town when it became the capital of the Republic of Texas. One visitor described it as a city of tents with only a couple of frame buildings. One of the frame buildings was the capitol building the Allen brothers built at the corner of Texas and Main. The Allens promised the government free use of this building as long as the government remained in Houston. President Houston's residence was a log cabin a few blocks away. It had two rooms and a lean-to at the back. Naturalist John James Audubon visited the new capital shortly after it was established and someone took him to see the president. Audubon later wrote that President Houston and Surgeon General Ashbel Smith were sharing one of the cluttered rooms in the official residence and the president's two black servants were living in the lean-to at the back. This cabin apparently was on Caroline at Preston. The president was not complaining. He wrote in 1838 that Houston had improved more than any place he knew anything about. He said new people were moving in at the rate of 200 a month.

The advertising the Allen brothers did alleged that ships could sail from New Orleans or New York to Houston without obstacles. Many people disputed this claim; so the Allens staged a demonstration. They engaged the captain of the steamboat *Laura* to make a trip from Columbia to Houston in January, 1837, and they invited several distinguished Texans to ride along. The *Laura* was the smallest steamboat in Texas waters at the time; she was just 89 feet long. The *Laura* took three days to travel from Harrisburg to Houston. The distinguished passengers were called upon several times to help clear away logs and obstructions, but several steamboats were making regular trips to Houston within a year after that demonstration.

John Kirby Allen died in 1838. Augustus and his wife, Charlotte, split up in 1850 and Augustus left Texas for good. He died in the East in 1864. Charlotte stayed and dominated Houston society for 45 years. The original Allen promotional fever had infected the four other Allen brothers and enough other early Houston settlers to ensure that Houston would survive.

Houston had two two-story houses, a warehouse and a

Top: *Charlotte Allen had a disagreement with her husband, Augustus, over the division of the family's assets after John Allen died. They separated. Augustus moved away, but Charlotte stayed in Houston. She was a pillar of the community into the 20th century. One of the more imposing monuments in Glenwood Cemetery marks her grave.*

Center: *The government of the republic bought a small store building at Main and Preston and converted it into a residence for the chief executive in 1838. This first White House was on the site where the Scanlan Building is today. President Houston lived in a small log cabin on Caroline before the government acquired this building.*

Bottom: *The first shopping center in Houston looked like this. The Harris County Heritage Society's shops on Bagby Street occupy a frame building that is a replica of a row of commercial establishments originally built in 1837 on the west side of Main Street between Preston and Congress.*

hotel by the end of 1837. One of the two-story houses was the A.C. Briscoe home at Main and Prairie. Briscoe was a veteran of the Battle of San Jacinto and the first county judge here. The first warehouse was at Main and Commerce, backing up to the bayou. The first hotel was at Travis and Franklin where the Southern Pacific building is now. The hotel was built by Ben Fort Smith and operated by George Wilson.

Harrisburg had been the original administrative center of Harris County. The town was founded in 1824 by John Richardson Harris. The county was originally called Harrisburg County. The county seat was moved to Houston shortly after Houston was established. The name of the county was changed then to Harris. The first courthouse in Houston was a double log cabin and the original jail was a crude log building with no windows or doors. There was only a trap door in the roof. The original courthouse and jail were on the same block where the Harris County Civil Courthouse is today.

One of the capital city's prominent female citizens was locked up in the log jail and put on trial for her life in the log courthouse in 1839. Pamelia Mann had borrowed some money from a man named Hardy to finance a boarding house at Washington-on-the-Brazos during the convention that produced the Texas Declaration of Independence. Hardy died and his widow demanded that the money be repaid to her. Pamelia produced a receipt purporting to show that she had repaid most of the loan before Hardy died. The widow denounced the receipt as a forgery and filed charges.

Pamelia Mann had built another boarding house by the time the case came to trial. She was operating the Mansion House at Congress and Milam. She was kept in jail during the trial because of the seriousness of the charge against her.

Forged land titles were among the most serious problems Texans had to deal with during the early days of the republic. The first Congress of the Republic accordingly had passed a law making forgery a capital offense. The penalty was hanging. The jury found Pamelia Mann guilty of forging the receipt. The jury recommended mercy, but the judge followed the law and sentenced Mrs. Mann to death. The jury petitioned President Mirabeau Lamar to commute the sentence. He did more than commute it; Lamar issued a presidential pardon to Mrs. Mann and she went back to her boarding house.

Saving Pamelia Mann from the hangman was about the last official act Mirabeau Lamar performed as president in

Above left: *The Harrisburg section of east Houston was a town before Houston was established. John R. Harris settled here in 1823. The town and the county were named for him. This marker is on the site at Lawndale and Broadway where the Harrisburg Bank is today.*

Above right: *The Texas constitution did not allow consecutive terms for the president; so Texans had to choose a new president when Sam Houston's first term ended. They chose Mirabeau B. Lamar. Lamar moved the government to Austin. There Congress met in a log building while President Lamar lived in a stylish house.*

Houston. Lamar was the son of a Georgia planter. He came to Texas in 1835. He performed heroically the duties Sam Houston assigned to him at the Battle of San Jacinto and was elected vice president when Houston was elected president in 1836.

Opponents and critics of Sam Houston rallied around Lamar in the second presidential election in 1838. Houston could not run again because the constitution of the republic prohibited a president from serving consecutive terms. Peter W. Grayson and James Collinsworth were the only other candidates. Grayson shot himself and Collinsworth drowned himself before the election. Lamar was the only living candidate on the ballot on election day. He took over the president's office in December, 1838.

The new administration declared war on the Indians, threatened the Mexicans and started looking for ways to get the government out of the town named for Sam Houston. Lamar wanted to move the capital to the site on the Colorado where the city of Austin is today and he got the Congress to go along with him. The government hired contractors to build a new town on the Colorado. They built the capitol with logs, but the Executive Mansion was a proper two-story frame house painted white.

The Allen brothers put a sign in the window of the old capitol building in Houston, offering it for rent. It was vacant about a month before it was rented and turned into a hotel. The Capitol Hotel operated in the original capitol building until 1881 when Abraham Groesbeeck bought it and tore it down. He built a new brick hotel in its place and gave it the same name. Groesbeeck went broke and William Marsh Rice bought the new hotel at a tax sale. William Marsh Rice had come to Texas from Massachusetts in 1838 with a little money he had made from a store he owned there. Rice settled in Houston in 1839 and opened a store. He eventually became one of Houston's most prominent citizens.

Houston had several permanent buildings, a school and a couple of theaters by this time, but some people thought the town was bound to die after the government moved away. Andrew Briscoe was convinced that Harrisburg had a brighter future; so he moved there. An outbreak of yellow fever discouraged people from moving to Houston and a couple of wrecked ships blocked the bayou between Houston and Harrisburg, but the town never came close to dying. Houston had a population of 2,000 in 1840. Merchants and shippers formed the Buffalo Bayou Company to raise money to remove the sunken ships and other obstacles from the bayou. Business leaders got the Congress to grant them a charter for a chamber of commerce to promote the city and the port.

There was some question about the legality of the Buffalo Bayou Company's moving sunken ships since they were private property. Congress cleared up the question in 1842 by granting Houston specific authority to have disabled ships and any other obstructions moved out of the channel. The Congress at the same time granted the city the right to levy fees on shipping to raise money for improvements to the channel.

The founder of the school that became Rice University came to Houston in 1838. William Marsh Rice was murdered in New York by some associates bent on taking for themselves the fortune he had earmarked for the school.

Houstonians now began forming churches. The First Methodist was organized first. The Allen brothers donated half a block of land for it on Texas Avenue where the Houston Chronicle Building is today. The First Presbyterian congregation met in the capitol building until the Presbyterian Church was built at Main and Capitol in 1842. The Episcopalians organized a church in 1839, but they didn't build their first building at Texas and Fannin until 1845. The First Baptist Church was organized in 1841 with its original building at Texas and Travis. The first Catholic church acquired a site at Franklin and Caroline in 1841.

The principal newspaper was the *Telegraph and Texas Register*. Gail Borden and his brother Thomas started the paper in San Felipe in 1835. They moved it to Harrisburg during the panic in 1836. Mexican troops seized the press in Harrisburg and threw it into the bayou. The *Telegraph and Texas Register* suspended publication until the Bordens could get another press. The Bordens resumed publication in Columbia in time to cover the first meeting of

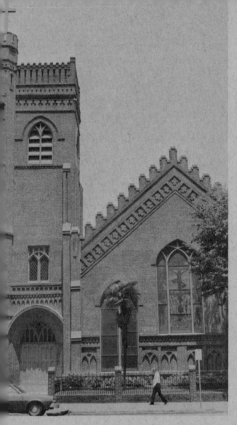

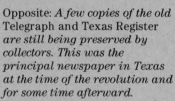

Opposite: *A few copies of the old Telegraph and Texas Register are still being preserved by collectors. This was the principal newspaper in Texas at the time of the revolution and for some time afterward.*

Above left: *Christ Church Cathedral still occupies the site on Texas Avenue between Fannin and San Jacinto where the first Episcopal church was built. This building was built in 1893 and was badly damaged by fire in 1938.*

Right: *The Annunciation Catholic Church at Crawford and Texas was built in 1874. The steeple was designed by Galveston architect Nicholas Clayton and added in 1881.*

the Congress of the Republic there. The Bordens sold their paper to Jacob Cruger and Francis Moore when the government of the republic left Columbia. The new owners brought the paper to Houston, where they stayed when the government moved on to Austin.

The *Telegraph and Texas Register* changed hands several times and went out of business in 1873. A new owner revived it as the *Houston Telegraph* in 1874, but it closed down for good in 1878. The *Telegraph and Texas Register* was not the first Texas newspaper, but it was the first one to publish more than just a few issues.

The government of the republic moved back to Houston briefly in 1842. Sam Houston had been elected president again and he never favored Austin as the capital. The Mexicans made a couple of forays into San Antonio and President Houston used those as an excuse to close down Austin. The old capitol building at Texas and Main was a hotel by this time; so the Senate had to meet in the Odd Fellows' Hall. The House met in the new First Presbyterian Church at Main and Capitol until the government moved on to Washington-on-the-Brazos. It stayed there until Texas joined the Union in 1845.

Houston had organized a city government with a mayor and eight aldermen by 1840. The city was divided into four wards. Each ward elected two aldermen. The First Ward was everything north of Congress and west of Main. The Second Ward was everything north of Congress and east of Main. The Third Ward was everything south of Congress and east of Main. The Fourth Ward was south of Congress and west of Main. The Fifth Ward and Sixth Ward were added later as development spread north of Buffalo Bayou. The wards ceased to exist as political subdivisions many years ago, but the terms are still used to describe the black ghettos in the areas near downtown.

Stage lines linked Houston with Austin, Richmond and Washington-on-the-Brazos by the early 1840s. The first cotton compress was established in 1844. The first sawmill was established on Buffalo Bayou at Milam Street about the same time. A cornmeal mill on the bayou at Texas Avenue was using three oxen on a treadmill for power. The city extended from the bayou on the north to Walker Street on the south, from Bagby on the west to Caroline on the east, in 1842. The city limits were extended a little later to cover nine square miles. English writer William Bollaert observed that Houstonians all slept under mosquito bars in the summers because the mosquitos were so bad.

The 1850 Census was the first one after Texas joined the Union. It showed Houston's population as 2,397. Galveston

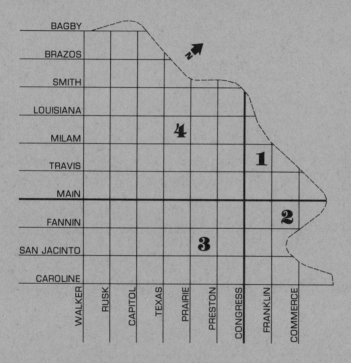

The original political organization of Houston divided the town into four wards. Each ward was entitled to two aldermen in the beginning.

was the biggest city in the state and the port there was getting most of the business Houston coveted. Most ships could not make it over the sand bars to get into Buffalo Bayou. They stopped at the Galveston docks or else unloaded their cargoes onto barges. Only barges and small ships were calling at Houston.

The legislature appropriated money for the first time in 1853 for improvements to the Houston channel. The appropriation was only $4,000. But the lawmakers voted another $45,000 in 1857 to cut channels through Redfish Reef and Clopper's Bar to allow bigger ships to enter the Houston channel. Most of the boats operating in the Houston channel at that time were owned by the Houston Navigation Company. The company was a syndicate of Houston businessmen including William Marsh Rice. Houston Navigation charged $2 or $3 a head for passengers and 50 cents a bale for cotton.

William Marsh Rice was one of the leading citizens in Houston by this time. He and Ebenezer Nichols had one of

Opposite: *The founders intended that Houston should be a major seaport, but Houston is 50 miles from the sea. Ships of any size reached the Houston docks only with great difficulty in the early years. Houstonians started improving the channel in the 1840s. The improvements have been continuing ever since.*

Above: *The former home of William Marsh Rice is one of the historic buildings the Harris County Heritage Society maintains in Sam Houston Park. Rice's business partner, Ebenezer Nichols, was building this house in 1850 when Rice and Margaret Bremond married. The Rices bought the building from Nichols. They* completed it and lived in it until Margaret died in 1863. The Heritage Society conducts tours of the restored historic buildings in Sam Houston Park.

84

the biggest stores on Main Street. Rice got interested in railroads after he married railroad promoter Paul Bremond's daughter Margaret in 1850. The first railroad was the line the Buffalo Bayou, Brazos and Colorado built from Harrisburg to Stafford in 1853. Rice had stock in it and he also invested in Bremond's Houston and Texas Central in 1856.

The Lutherans organized their first Houston church in 1851 and the first iron foundry began making kettles for the sugar plantations.

The city of Houston acquired its own dredge boat in 1856 and put it to work on the bayou. Sixty thousand bales of Texas cotton went to market in 1858 through the Port of Houston.

The Census of 1860 credited Houston with a population of 4,845. Fourteen Texas counties had more people than Harris County. The richest man in the county was William Marsh Rice and he was believed to be the second richest man in the state. Rice owned the biggest building in

Top: *Houston's hopes of turning Buffalo Bayou into a major port centered mostly on cotton in the beginning. Planters with access to the Brazos River could ship their cotton out by barge and steamer. Most of that cotton went through Galveston. Planters in the area north of Houston had to haul their cotton to Houston by wagon and oxcart. The roads were so awful that Houston boosters were planning at one time to pave them with planks. The plank road idea was abandoned when Paul Bremond began building the Houston and Texas Central Railroad into the cotton belt in the 1850s.*

Center: *The earliest railroad in the area was the Buffalo Bayou, Brazos and Colorado between Harrisburg and Stafford. The*

first locomotive was the General Sherman. It was named for Sidney Sherman. He was a hero of the battle of San Jacinto and the founder of the Buffalo Bayou, Brazos and Colorado line.

Bottom: *One of the most prominent businessmen in Houston during the Civil War was T.W. House. He was a merchant and planter and he had some success at running ships through the Union blockade off the Texas coast. House produced and sold the first ice cream in Houston.*

Houston. One of his several businesses was hauling ice to Houston from New England by ship.

The first rail line between Houston and Galveston was completed in 1860. A telegraph link between the two cities had been completed a short time earlier. The telegraph line was kept operating all during the Civil War with sulphur water from Sour Lake. The batteries normally used sulphuric acid. None was available in Texas during the war because of the Union blockade, but some one discovered that the smelly water from Sour Lake made a reasonable substitute. Five short rail lines operated out of Houston by the time the Civil War began.

The 1860 Census also showed a total of 1,068 slaves in Houston. All were not owned by planters. William Marsh Rice owned 15 of them. Most of the people in the city at that time came from the Old South. Sentiment here was strongly in favor of secession. The vote in Harris County in February of 1861 was 1,084 for secession and 144 against.

Houston abolished all wharf charges just before the war started, trying to draw business away from the Port of Galveston. There was substantial traffic between the two ports during the war, but very little between them and points beyond because of the federal blockade. Blockade runners made big profits from cargoes they managed to slip past the Union ships. Some of the blockade runners operated out of Houston. One of them was owned by merchant T.W. House. He was the father of Edward M. House, later to be assistant to President Woodrow Wilson.

Sam Houston was governor of Texas in 1861. He did everything he could to prevent secession, short of calling in the Union Army. President Abraham Lincoln sent word that such a call would be answered. Houston decided to try to prevail through reason, but it was not a time for reason. The Secession Convention of 1861 swept Houston out of office when he failed to appear to take the oath of allegiance to the Confederacy that the Convention had decided to require. Houston told everybody willing to listen that the South could not win the war. Other Texans were killed by vigilantes and bushwackers for making statements like that, but people seemed to think Sam Houston had earned the right to say anything he wanted to say and do anything he wanted to do. Sam Houston thought so, too. Confederate authorities put out an order at one stage during the war requiring all Texans to carry identification. Houston did not and would not do it. People said that a patrol stopped Sam Houston one day and asked for his identification. Houston supposedly bellowed that San Jacinto was his passport and he supposedly rode on without any further interference. It may have happened. It may have been a story somebody else started or it may have been a story Houston started. But it sounded to Texans like something Sam Houston might do. More people were beginning to believe Houston's predictions about the outcome of the war by the time he died in 1863.

Houstonians volunteered for Confederate forces as eagerly as they voted for secession. One thousand men turned out on September 9, 1861, to join Benjamin F. Terry in the cavalry regiment that became known as Terry's

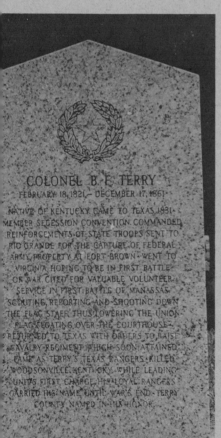

This tombstone in Glenwood Cemetery marks the grave of one of the first Texans to fight for the South in the Civil War. Benjamin F. Terry was a planter in Fort Bend County. He voted for secession as a delegate to the Secession Convention in 1861 and then went to Virginia to fight in the First Battle of Manassas. Terry came back to Houston and recruited the cavalry unit that came to be called Terry's Texas Rangers. Terry was killed while leading his Rangers in their first battle in December, 1861.

87

Texas Rangers. The Bayou City Guards, the Gentry Volunteers, the Houston Artillery and the Texas Grays were some of the other Confederate units recruited in Houston. Houston bartender Dick Dowling became an instant hero by leading a successful Confederate defense against a Union invasion attempt at Sabine Pass. There was no fighting in the immediate vicinity of Houston. The closest was in Galveston. A force of Union soldiers and sailors captured Galveston at the end of December, 1862. A couple of Buffalo Bayou steamboats joined the makeshift force Confederate General John B. Magruder organized to take the island back on New Year's Day, 1863. There were no more Union troops in Galveston until the occupation force arrived June 19, 1865. Houston was occupied the following day by the 114th Ohio Regiment and the 34th Iowa Regiment.

The process the North called "Reconstruction" was proceeding fairly uneventfully until 1867 when the U.S. Congress threw out the presidential plan for reassimilating the Southern states and put in its own, much harsher Reconstruction Program. The U.S. military governor of Texas removed the elected governor from office and arranged a new election. Union veteran Edmund J. Davis was chosen governor. He removed most local officials and replaced them with people loyal to the Union. Houston's elected mayor Alexander McGowen was removed and replaced with T.H. Scanlan in August, 1870. Four of the elected aldermen were removed and replaced with black Union sympathizers.

SACRED TO THE MEMORY OF
THIRTY TWO
CONFEDERATE SOLDIERS
DIED IN THEIR COUNTRY'S SERVIC
REST IN PEACE.

Opposite and above: *A number of Confederate veterans were buried in a city cemetery on the north side of Buffalo Bayou where Elder Street is today. The city built the original Jeff Davis public hospital on the cemetery grounds in 1924. A repair shop for the fire department has since been built on the same grounds, right alongside this marble slab the city installed in 1924 to atone for disturbing the veterans' graves.*

Right: *The Ancient Order of Hibernians commissioned this statue of a son of County Galway. Richard W. (Dick) Dowling was a saloonkeeper in Houston before and after the Civil War. He was a lieutenant in the Confederate Army during the war. He thwarted a Union attempt to invade Texas at the Battle of Sabine Pass. Dowling Street was named for him. His statue originally stood in Market Square, but was moved later to Sam Houston Park. It stands now in Hermann Park. The Hibernians give it a bath every St. Patrick's Day.*

Many freed slaves had moved to Houston. They settled in what they called Freedmantown on the outer edge of the Fourth Ward, where the Allen Parkway Village public housing is today.

B.A. Shepherd and T.M. Bagby organized the First National Bank in 1866. The first trolley cars appeared on Houston streets in 1868. They were pulled by mules. The first gaslights were installed the same year and the city's first ice plant opened the next year. Galveston got the lion's share of the maritime business when ships started running regularly again. Galveston would continue to be the dominant port into the 1890s and grow very rich while Houston struggled to overcome its natural disadvantages. Houston businessmen took a step in the right direction in 1869 when they formed the Buffalo Bayou Ship Channel Company to dredge the channel to a depth of 9 feet.

The Congress of the United States designated Houston a port in 1870. The Census of 1870 gave Houston a population of 9,332. Harris County had a population of 17,375.

Only Washington County had more people at the time.

The population of Galveston was substantially larger than Houston's. The Port of Galveston was doing much more business than the Port of Houston, but the only rail line out of Galveston came through Houston; so shipments between Galveston and the interior were subject to handling charges in Houston. Galveston bankers and merchants formed the Gulf, Colorado and Santa Fe Railroad and built a line into the interior that passed well to the west of Houston through Sugarland. Business at the Port of Galveston got even better, but cotton farmers were beginning to grumble about the freight charges and wharf rates.

The first synagogue in the city was established on Franklin Street in 1870. The City Bank of Houston opened the same year. It closed in 1885.

Congress approved $10,000 for improvements to the Houston Ship Channel in the early 1870s. The Buffalo Bayou Ship Channel Company started dredging a channel across Morgan's Point, but the work was interrupted by the financial panic of 1873.

Mayor Scanlan and the carpetbag city government decided to tear down the old Houston City Hall and put up a fancy new city hall and market house on the same site. They annexed several additional miles of territory to get the tax base to support the bonds. The original plans called for a building to cost $250,000. Overruns and miscalculations brought the total to almost half a million. The building was only insured for $100,000 when it burned in 1876. The insurance company made some repairs, but the building

The United States Army removed from office in 1867 all officials involved in any way with the Confederate cause. The deposed officials were replaced by people Union authorities considered more "reliable." The new officials were called "carpetbaggers" by the Southerners because many of them had come down from the North with only what possessions they could carry in a carpetbag. T.H. Scanlan was the man chosen to replace the elected mayor of Houston. Scanlan had lived in Houston before the war. He spent the war years in Mexico. He was not technically a carpetbagger, but to old Houstonians he was the carpetbag mayor. Scanlan served until the Reconstruction period ended in 1874.

burned again a few years later. Scanlan was gone from the mayor's office long before that. The Reconstruction period ended in Texas in 1874 when Richard Coke won the governor's office from Edmund J. Davis. Coke put people of the old school back in office in the cities. He appointed James T.D. Wilson to succeed Scanlan as mayor of Houston in January, 1874. Scanlan left the city with a debt of $1.4 million and no credit rating. The city's bond holders were getting restless.

T.W. House opened a new bank in 1873 and it closed in 1907.

The Houston Light Guard was organized in 1873 to compete in military events. There had been two similar volunteer groups before the Civil War. They had both disbanded and the members had joined various fighting units for the war. But the Houston Light Guard stayed together and fought as a unit in several wars.

The Houston Savings Bank opened in 1874 and closed in 1886.

The Houston Board of Trade and Cotton Exchange was organized in 1874. The organization started very small in rented space, but it grew as the cotton business grew. The board was reorganized in 1877 as the Houston Cotton Exchange and Board of Trade.

The Port of Galveston and the Morgan Steamship Line fell out over wharf fees in 1874. Galveston had not been charging this good customer any fees before then. Owner Charles Morgan was very displeased when the fees were imposed. Morgan had dredged his own channel and

Opposite top: *The first building built by the Houston Cotton Exchange and Board of Trade is still in use. It was built in 1884 at the corner of Franklin and Travis. The old Cotton Exchange was restored in 1973 and several professional people have offices in it now.*

Opposite bottom: *The Houston Light Guard was organized in 1873 to compete in parades and drills and to fight when fighting was necessary. The guard won a lot of prizes and built this armory at Caroline and Truxillo in 1925. The guard donated the armory to the Texas National Guard in 1939.*

93

Left: *Telephones looked like this in 1880 when Houston got its first telephone exchange. The white button set off a bell to signal the operator. The receiver was also the transmitter.*

Below: *The Morgan Steamship Line took exception to Galveston wharf charges in the 1870s and developed a new terminal on the Houston Ship Channel. The terminal on the north bank of the channel was called Clinton. Morgan ships linked up here with the Southern Pacific Railroad. Little is left of Clinton now except a dilapidated dock.*

established the Port of Morgan City in Louisiana a little earlier after a similar row with the Port of New Orleans. He handled the Galveston problem the same way. He took over the dredging on Morgan's Point and dredged a channel up Buffalo Bayou to Sims Bayou. He dredged a turning basin there and called it Clinton. Morgan built a rail line to connect his docks at Clinton with the major railroads in Houston. He then had a port he could use without paying wharf fees to Galveston or anyone else. Also he could charge other ships a fat fee for using his channel across Morgan's Point. The Morgan terminal at Clinton started operating in 1876. It didn't help Galveston. Congress appropriated $75,000 for more improvements to the Houston channel that year. The first grain elevator was established on the channel the next year.

Harris County had several free public schools by 1873. The first free public schools were established in Houston in 1877. They were supported by the state and administered by the city government until the Houston Independent School District was established in 1924.

A state fair was held in Houston each year between 1871 and 1878. The fairgrounds were west of South Main Street between about Hadley and Elgin. Interest in the fair dwindled in the late 1870s. The show was discontinued and the land was subdivided.

Mayor James Wilson and the city council gave a private contractor a franchise to build a water system for Houston in 1878. Citizens had depended upon shallow wells and cisterns up to that time. The contractor built a dam on Buffalo Bayou at Preston Street and a pipeline system to deliver bayou water to homes and business buildings. There were complaints about the quality of the water almost from the start. A few citizens drilled wells and found good artesian water fairly close to the surface. The franchise holder got discouraged and offered the Houston Water Works for sale. A Houston group bought the system. Former mayor Scanlan became president. He drilled some wells and tried to deliver only well water to households, but the bayou water his company was furnishing to industries and fire hydrants kept getting mixed up with the good water. The city bought out the system in 1906, drilled more wells and quit using water from the bayou.

Several other Texas counties grew more between 1870 and 1880 then Harris County did. The Census of 1880 showed a population of 16,513 for Houston and 27,985 for Harris County. Grayson, Dallas, Bexar and Fayette counties all had more people than Harris County.

The first telephone exchange was installed in Houston in 1880. There were 50 telephones. Long distance service didn't begin until 1895.

The railroad was completed between Houston and New Orleans in 1880 and through rail service between Houston and the West Coast began in 1882.

Congress made further appropriations for improvements to the Houston Ship Channel in 1880, 1881 and 1882, but Galveston continued to be the leading port. Houston and Galveston both were using quarantines by this time to divert business away from each other. The ostensible reason for the quarantines was yellow fever. All the coastal areas had outbreaks fairly regularly. Dr. Carlos Finlay of Cuba first suggested in 1881 that the fever was spread by the Aedes aegypti mosquito. But residents of the Gulf Coast consumed tons more quinine before a U.S. Army Commission headed by Dr. Walter Reed finally proved the mosquito theory in 1900 and started to develop some control measures.

The Houston Electric Light Company was organized in 1882 and the first electric street lights were turned on in

Opposite top: *This is one of the light company's early generating plants, photographed about 1900. The company that became Houston Lighting and Power was founded in 1882. Electric street lights began replacing the gaslights in 1884. This generator burned oil.*

Opposite bottom: *A new hotel was built in 1881 on the site where the capitol building had stood. This brick building at Texas and Main was called the Capitol Hotel when William Marsh Rice bought it. He kept the original name, but the trustees of his estate changed the name to Rice Hotel after Rice was killed.*

1884. The Houston Gas Company bought out Houston Electric Light and organized the present light company in 1894.

More than 20 newspapers started publishing in Houston between 1865 and 1880. Most of them lasted only a short time. A paper called *The Houston Post* began publishing in 1880 and folded in 1884. The present *Houston Post* was born in 1885 when the morning *Chronicle* and the evening *Journal* combined and took the name *Houston Post*. Ross Sterling bought this paper in 1924. He merged it with the *Houston Dispatch* and published it as the *Houston Post Dispatch* until he sold it to J.E. Josey in the 1930s. Josey changed the name back to *Houston Post*. Former governor William P. Hobby bought controlling interest in the *Post* in 1939 and it is still owned by his family.

W.H. Bailey started the *Houston Herald* in 1884. Marcellus E. Foster started publishing the *Houston Chronicle* in 1901. Foster bought the *Herald* in 1902 and published a combined paper he called the *Houston Chronicle and Herald*. The name was shortened to *Houston Chronicle* and Foster traded a half interest in the paper to Jesse Jones in 1908 as part payment for the building Jones built for the *Chronicle* that year. Jones bought out Foster's remaining interest in 1926. The present publisher is Jones's Houston Endowment, Incorporated, and that 1908 building is incorporated in the present Chronicle Building.

The Commercial National Bank opened in 1886 and merged into the South Texas National in 1912. The Houston National Bank opened in 1889. It was reorganized as the Houston National Exchange Bank in 1909.

The mayors of Houston during the 1880s were W.R. Baker and D.C. Smith. They managed to work out a compromise settlement with the investors holding the bonds the city's Reconstruction administration had issued. Houston voters set the stage for compromise by voting to pay the holders of the city's bonds no more than 50 cents on the dollar. The investors came out a little better than that in the final settlement and the city's credit rating began to improve.

Above: *The Sisters of Charity of the Incarnate Word established the first general hospital in 1887 at Caroline and Franklin. St. Joseph's Infirmary had 40 beds. It was the forerunner of the present St. Joseph Hospital complex.*

Right: *The first paving in Houston was not a city project. The merchants in the two blocks of Main Street nearest the bayou put up the money to have these two blocks paved with cut limestone.*

Left: *John Henry Kirby was one of the first people to exploit the East Texas pine forests. He founded the Kirby Lumber Company and the Kirby Petroleum Company.*

Above: *Kirby lived here at Smith and Gray in a Victorian house when he first moved to Houston in 1890. He remodelled the house and turned it into this brick and stone mansion. This house was occupied by the Houston Chapter of the Red Cross for many years. It was restored by the oil company that now occupies it. Party leaders worked out some of the strategy for the 1928 Democratic National Convention at meetings here in Kirby's house.*

Opposite: *The first electric street cars were a big improvement over the old mule cars, but they did not offer much protection from the weather.*

Some fancy steamboats were operating on Buffalo Bayou between Houston and Galveston by this time. The *Diana* and the *T.M. Bagby* were described as floating palaces equal to anything operating on the Mississippi.

The Sisters of Charity of the Incarnate Word opened the first hospital in Houston at Franklin and Caroline in 1887.

The Census of 1890 gave Texas a population of more than two million. Seven counties had more people than Harris County. Houston was credited with 27,557 people.

Congress started spending substantial sums of money on the Port of Galveston in the 1890s. There was an appropriation of $6 million to pay for the jetties at the channel entrance. The jetties were just as helpful to Houston traffic as they were to Galveston traffic. But the Congress also put up money to deepen the channel to the Galveston docks. The channel was dredged down to 14 feet in 1893, to 18 feet in 1895 and then to 25 feet in 1896. Most ships could then steam right up to the docks. It was a big plus for Galveston.

Retiring Congressman J.C. Hutcheson of Houston proposed a survey for a 25-foot channel to Houston. Representative Thomas Ball succeeded Hutcheson and he wangled an appointment to the Committee on Rivers and Harbors and got the 25-foot channel for Houston approved. But Congress made only token appropriations until the great hurricane of 1900 caused serious misgivings about the future of the Port of Galveston.

Charles Morgan died and in 1890 the federal government bought the Morgan Line's channel across Morgan's

Point. Tolls were abolished and the channel was opened to all ships. It was a plus for Houston, but the bigger ships still had to go to Galveston.

John Henry Kirby moved to Houston from Tyler County in 1890. Kirby was a lawyer. He won some cases for forest owners and he went into the timber business himself in a big way. He was the richest man in Houston by 1900.

The first electric street cars appeared in Houston in 1891. Twelve rail lines operated in and out of the city by this time and Houston was the most important rail center in the state.

The city had several packing houses and manufacturing plants by 1894. Barbed wire, brick, tile, cigars, textiles, carriages, wagons and beer were some of the products being made here.

Jacob Binz put up the first skyscraper in 1894 at the corner of Main and Texas across from the Capitol Hotel. The hotel was five stories then. The new Binz Building was a towering six stories. That original Binz Building was torn

Above: *Part of the old 1890s Magnolia Brewery has been turned into a restaurant. The brewery included an ice plant and occupied several buildings around the corner of Franklin and Milam. The brewery buildings extended out into Buffalo Bayou and some of the old brick work is still visible underneath the Franklin Street Bridge.*

Right: *The five-story Kiam Building was a showplace when it was finished in 1893. The building was built for Kiam's Clothiers. It had Houston's first electric elevator. Sakowitz occupied this building from 1918 to 1928.*

Opposite: *The corner of Main and Texas was one of the busiest intersections in town when Jacob Binz built this distinguished office building in 1894. This was the first six-story building in Houston. An 11-story glass building occupies the site now.*

Left: *Jesse H. Jones came to Houston from Dallas in 1899 and almost literally took over the town. He was a lumber merchant, builder and banker and the most influential person in Houston for a generation.*

Below: *Sam Houston Park behind the City Hall, where the Heritage Society's old houses are, was the first park acquired by the city. It was originally called City Park.*

down about 1950 and a two-story building built in its place. Eleven stories have since been added to that building and it is being called the Binz Building again.

The city's merchants and businessmen formed the Houston Business League in 1895 and this organization became the Houston Chamber of Commerce in 1910. The first city park was established in 1899. This was Sam Houston Park bound by Bagby, Walker and Dallas, where the Heritage Society's old houses are now. There was a small zoo when this was the only park in the city.

Jesse H. Jones moved to Houston in 1899 to manage a branch of his uncle's M.T. Jones Lumber Company. The Joneses had come to Texas from Tennessee when Jesse was nine. They settled in Dallas in 1883. What Jesse Jones might have done in Dallas we can only guess, but his contributions to Houston are history. He opened his own lumber business shortly after arriving in Houston and then went into building and later into banking. He became one of the biggest boosters of the city and the port. He did more than any other single individual to advance Houston's interests from the time he arrived until he died.

Jesse Jones believed in Houston and in real estate. He was associated with many rich and famous oilmen, but he was always dubious about their business. Jones invested $20,000 in the Humble Company when it was founded. He was pleased to be able to sell the stock and get out a year later. He doubled his money, but some other early stockholders made vast fortunes as Humble evolved into the giant Exxon, USA. ■

PART THREE

Houston 1900-1946

"Houston is booming. It is a live town. The commercial instinct is very strong."

John Millsaps, 1910.

The official population of Houston reached 44,633 in the Census of 1900. Harris County had a total population of 63,786. Dallas and Bexar counties both had more people.

Houstonians had 2,000 telephones in service in 1900. The Houston and Texas Central Railroad built the Grand Central depot that year off Washington Avenue near where the U.S. Post Office is now.

Andrew Carnegie gave the city $50,000 for a library building. The city provided the site at McKinney and Travis. The new Houston Lyceum and Carnegie Association took over the small library that had been accumulated by the Houston Lyceum since it was established in 1848. The first librarian in the new building was Julia Ideson.

The San Jacinto Chapter of the Daughters of the Republic of Texas was organized in 1901 to take care of the San Jacinto Battleground and put up markers. The battleground was the property of a widow named Peggy McCormick when the battle was fought. It was sold to various individuals after Mrs. McCormick died. The state bought the 10 acres around the site of the Texan cemetery in 1883 and bought 200 more acres in 1891. Smaller tracts have been added since then. The San Jacinto State Park now covers about 400 acres.

The oil discoveries at Spindletop in 1901, at Humble in 1905 and at Goose Creek in 1906 put Houston on the way to becoming the center of the oil and oil field equipment businesses. Two of the drillers active in southeast Texas after the Spindletop discovery were Howard R. Hughes and Walter Sharp. They became impatient with the drill bits

Major oil discoveries were being made all around the Houston area in the early 1900s. There was no thought of proration or spacing at the time. Oilmen crowded their rigs as close together as they could in the Humble field, here, and in all the other areas where they found oil.

available. Hughes perfected a bit that would cut through rock better than anything drillers had been able to get before. Hughes and Sharp formed the Sharp-Hughes Tool Company in Houston to manufacture the new bit. Hughes bought Sharp's interest after Sharp died in 1912. He ran the business as the Hughes Tool Company until he died in 1924. Then it passed to Howard R. Hughes, Jr.

The Texas Company moved its headquarters to Houston in 1908 because company president J.S. Cullinan was convinced Houston would become the capital of the oil industry.

Congress appropriated another million dollars for the Houston Ship Channel in 1902. The Turning Basin was completed in 1908.

Houston voters in 1904 approved an experiment with the commission form of government. The government was headed by a full-time mayor. Each of the four aldermen headed one of the city departments. H. Baldwin Rice was the first mayor to serve under this arrangement. He was a

Opposite: *Steel tycoon Andrew Carnegie built Houston a library. He built libraries all over the country, but he only paid for the buildings. The beneficiary cities had to supply the books. Houston luckily had some books. The Carnegie Library and Lyceum was several years old when this photograph was made. It stood on the corner of McKinney and Travis. Woolworth's now occupies the site — and all the rest of the block, too.*

Top: *Houston started the 20th century with a new railroad passenger depot. Grand Central Station was near the site of the present Southern Pacific depot, where passenger trains still stop occasionally.*

Right: *A town grew up on the edge of the battleground where Sam Houston defeated the Mexicans, but the town of San Jacinto was dead and gone before 1900. The state had started to acquire some of the land for the park that now includes an imposing stone monument and historical museum.*

111

112

Opposite top: *Houston leaders for a long time subscribed to the original Allen notion that the place for the port was at the foot of Main Street. This picture of the Main Street docks apparently was made about 1910. It had already been decided by then that the main docks and turning basin would be farther downstream, actually much closer to old Harrisburg than to Main Street.*

Opposite center: *Organized firefighting began in Houston in 1838 when Congress issued a charter to a volunteer bucket brigade organized by the residents. The firefighters were all volunteers until 1895 when they went on the city payroll. The Fire Department built a fancy central station in 1902 at Texas and San Jacinto. The city's last three fire horses were retired when the firemen moved from here in 1924 to the new central station at Caroline and Preston. The county now uses the 1924 building as a marshalling area for jurors. The old fire horses were given quarters at the Hermann Park Zoo and a fireman from the central station went out every day to feed them as long as they lived.*

Above: *No ships have called at the foot of Main Street for a long time. The original port area was landscaped and turned into Allen's Landing Park in the 1970s.*

Opposite bottom: *Joseph S. Cullinan moved to Houston in 1908 and brought his Texas Company with him. Cullinan had started the company that would become Texaco in Beaumont in 1903. He had earlier started a company in Corsicana that became Mobil. Cullinan was convinced Houston was the logical headquarters for the petroleum industry and his move helped make it happen. He became one of the big boosters of the city and the port.*

nephew of William Marsh Rice.

Carry Nation appeared in Houston in 1905 and caused about $750 damage to a saloon in the Fifth Ward. Carry was the most famous prohibitionist in the country. Her specialty was attacking saloons with an axe. She took her axe to the establishment in the Fifth Ward because the proprietor had named the place for her.

There were 80 automobiles on the streets of Houston by 1905. And that was the year young Oscar F. Holcombe moved to Houston from Alabama. Holcombe went into the construction and contracting business and prospered. He ran for mayor in 1920. He was elected and he served as mayor off and on for the next 35 years. Holcombe served a total of 11 terms.

The Union National Bank was formed in 1905 from the merger of the Union Bank and Trust and the Merchants' National Bank. The Lumbermen's National Bank opened in 1907. Bankers' Trust opened in 1908 with Jesse Jones as chairman. The Great Southern Insurance Company was founded the following year.

The population of Houston was up to 78,800 in the 1910 Census. Harris County's population was 115,693. Dallas and Bexar counties still had more people.

The Union Railroad Station opened in 1910 and made the corner of Texas and Crawford one of the busiest intersections in town.

Congress voted that year to approve a Houston plan for completing and maintaining the Houston Ship Channel. A delegation of citizens had visited Washington in 1909 to

Opposite: *Prohibitionist Carry Nation came to Houston in 1905 to wreck a saloon with her axe. She was living in Kansas at the time, but she was no stranger here. Carry and her husband had lived in Columbia and Richmond, Texas, in the 1890s. He was a correspondent for the Houston Post for a time.*

Right: *Former mayor T.H. Scanlan left his spinster daughters very well fixed when he died. The Scanlan sisters spent part of their legacy for an office building they regarded as a monument to him. The Scanlan Building was completed in 1909 at the corner of Main and Preston, where Sam Houston once lived. It was the finest building in town when it was new. The Scanlan building was renovated and modernized in 1981.*

Bottom: *The County Commissioners put up this courthouse in 1910 on the same block of land the founders originally set aside for the courthouse. Courts and county departments now occupy eight other buildings surrounding the original courthouse square. The cupola on top of this building looks as though it was designed to have a statue on top, but it never did.*

Above: *County employees are working in one building county officials never intended to occupy. The county government bought the old Sweeney, Coombs Building at Main and Congress along with all the other property on this block in the 1970s. The original intention was to tear down all the buildings to make way for the new County Administration Building (visible behind the old building here). But conservationists made such a fuss that the county commissioners agreed to save this old building and one next door to it. The Sweeney, Coombs Building has been restored, but the county has never done anything with the building next door and probably won't.*

Opposite: *An interurban trolley operated between downtown Houston and downtown Galveston for 25 years, beginning in 1911. If such a service existed today nearly everyone would favor keeping it. But nearly everyone was convinced in 1936 when the interurban was abandoned that the private automobile was the best way to get around.*

116

propose that Houston and the U.S. government split the cost.

The Texas legislature created the Navigation District and the district put a proposal for a bond issue to a public vote. The voters approved an issue of $1.4 million for channel improvements. Investors were not enthusiastic about buying the bonds, so Jesse Jones rounded up the leading bankers and persuaded them that the Houston banks ought to buy the port bonds. Several arrangements for managing the port were tried before the city and the county agreed on the present Port of Houston Authority. There are five commissioners. The city names two, the county names two and the city and county jointly choose the chairman.

Houston had 15 miles of electric street car lines by 1910 and 190 miles of paved streets. Electric interurban cars began running between Houston and Galveston in 1911. There were 18 cars a day. The tracks followed approximately the route of the present Gulf Freeway. The trip took

about an hour each way. The service continued until 1936 when it was scrapped because most people by that time were traveling by car.

Scripps-Howard started publishing the *Houston Press* in 1911. It was a lively afternoon paper, smaller and much less reverent than the *Post* and the *Chronicle*. Several of the paper's writers became local celebrities, but the paper never was a commercial success. Scripps-Howard sold it to the *Chronicle* in 1964 and the *Chronicle* shut it down.

Rice Institute started classes in September, 1912. This was the school that later became Rice University. It was provided for in a will William Marsh Rice wrote before he was killed in New York in 1900, but legal complications delayed its opening. Rice's second wife had written a second will before she died, purporting to give to others some of the property she and Rice had set aside for the institute. Also a New York lawyer had forged a will purporting to give him a large part of the property Rice had set aside for the institute. That lawyer eventually was convicted of influencing an associate to kill Rice with chloroform. That ended the lawyer's claim. The trustees Rice had designated to manage his estate and his institute made a settlement with the second Mrs. Rice's heirs. They had about $4.5 million in assets left for the institute, including the Capitol Hotel. They changed the name of the hotel to The Rice Hotel and leased it to Jesse Jones. He demolished the building and put up a new Rice Hotel. It opened in 1913.

One of the original Rice trustees was Rice's lawyer,

Opposite top: *Several members of the staff of the* Houston Press *went on to distinguished careers elsewhere when the* Press *sold out to the* Chronicle *in 1964. Popular author Thomas Thompson stopped by the abandoned building on Chartres during a visit in 1982. He was city editor here once. He says it was the best job he ever had.*

Opposite bottom: *Rice University exists because William Marsh Rice willed it and because he had a good lawyer. Rice was murdered and the killers almost made off with the fortune Rice had earmarked for the school.*

118

James A. Baker. He apparently deserves most of the credit for exposing the New York lawyer's plot and for holding the Rice estate together. He was the son of one of the founders of the Baker and Botts law firm and the grandfather of President Ronald Reagan's aide, James A. Baker III.

The United States built a new Post Office building in Houston in 1912. This was the building in the 700 block of San Jacinto now called the Customs House. The post office moved to a new building off Washington Avenue in the 1960s.

The Houston Symphony Orchestra was established in 1913. It has been directed at different times since then by such luminaries as Leopold Stokowski, Sir John Barbirolli, Ernst Hoffman, Efrem Kurtz and Andre Previn.

The 25-foot channel to the Turning Basin was completed in 1914. President Woodrow Wilson took part in the dedication November 10. The president pressed a button in Washington that set off a cannon at the port. That was the official opening, but ships were not lined up waiting to get

Opposite: *Jesse Jones started with a lumber yard and developed a chain of lumber yards before he got into building. Jones built the present Rice Hotel in 1913 partly because he wanted a nice place downtown to live.*

Top: *The distinguished building on San Jacinto that is now called the U.S Customs House was built in 1912 to serve as the Main Post Office for Houston. Generations of recruits and draftees passed through the Armed Forces Induction Center here.*

Right: *The Induction Center here was the place where heavyweight champion Mohammed Ali declined to be drafted for Vietnam in 1966. The Supreme Court eventually upheld Ali's position in 1971.*

Above: *Regular steamship service did not begin until nine months after the port was completed. Business improved after the steamer* Satilla *made her first visit to the port in 1915.*

Left: *J.S. Cullinan resigned from the Texas Company in 1914 and formed the American Republics Company. Cullinan built a new building on Texas Avenue east of Main Street to house his new company. An insurance company owns it now, but this was called the Petroleum Building in Cullinan's day. Cullinan developed a custom of flying the Jolly Roger from the top of this building every Saint Patrick's Day. The Ku Klux Klan was active then. Cullinan was an Irish Catholic. He flew the skull and crossbones to defy the bigots.*

Opposite: *Two rich bachelors gave the Texas Medical Center its start. George Hermann made his money in real estate and oil. He instructed the executors of his estate to build and operate a hospital. They built Hermann Hospital.*

into the Houston Ship Channel. The war in Europe had reduced ocean commerce drastically. But Houstonians were able to persuade the Southern Steamship Company to schedule regular service between Houston and New York. This called for another celebration. A Deep Water Jubilee was scheduled to coincide with the expected arrival of the Southern Steamship Company's steamer *Satilla*. There would have been free barbecue and a lot of speeches at the Turning Basin if the *Satilla* had arrived when she was supposed to on August 19, 1915. But the ship was delayed in the Gulf by the great 1915 hurricane. About 2,000 people turned out to welcome her when she did arrive on August 22, but it was not the jubilee it was meant to be.

The first oil refinery had been built on the channel by this time. Two or three other oil companies were looking at possible refinery sites.

The Texas Company completed a new headquarters building on Rusk between Fannin and San Jacinto in 1914. J.S. Cullinan left the Texas Company and a little later established the American Republics Oil Company.

George Hermann died in the fall of 1914. He was a bachelor with no close relatives. Houston was his beneficiary. George Hermann's parents had come to Houston sometime before 1840. He told people they arrived with $5. His mother pawned her jewelry to raise money to start a bakery and they prospered. George Hermann inherited substantial real estate when they died. He bought more land and some of the land he bought turned out to have oil under it. He grew rich but not extravagant. Shortly before he died, Hermann gave the city 285 acres of land off South Main where he once had operated a sawmill. That gift was the nucleus of Hermann Park. Hermann left the city the downtown block where the City Hall Reflection Pool is now. He left the balance of his estate in a foundation to build and maintain a hospital. Hermann Hospital opened in 1925.

The Anderson Clayton Company of Oklahoma opened a branch office in Houston in 1907. The company was founded by Frank and M.D. Anderson and Ben and Will Clayton. They were cotton brokers. They moved their headquarters to Houston in 1916 and became the biggest cotton dealers in the world. M.D. Anderson headed the company until he died in 1939.

J.S. Cullinan donated a tract of land at Montrose and South Main to the Houston Art League for a museum in 1917. The Museum of Fine Arts was established on the property in 1924.

James A. Elkins moved to Houston from Huntsville in 1917. He served as district attorney briefly during World War I. He started a law practice after the war with William Vinson and then went in with J.W. Keeland in a bank that eventually became the First City National.

The Humble Company was chartered in 1917.

The U.S. Army established two training bases in Houston for World War I. Ellington Field trained pilots and bombardiers for the Air Corps. It was named for one of the air age's early casualties, Lt. Eric Ellington. Camp Logan was originally a National Guard base. The Army took it over and turned it into an emergency training center for troops going overseas. A National Guard unit from Illinois was moved to Houston to guard the base while it was being built. The enlisted men in this unit were all black and they could not adjust to the way black people were treated in Houston.

City police arrested one of the black privates on August 23, 1917, for shooting dice. The police then arrested and jailed a black M.P. when he inquired about the case. A rumor got back to the camp that the M.P. had been killed.

124

Top: *M.D. Anderson was one of the founders of the Anderson Clayton Company. He gave the trustees of his estate considerable latitude in determining how to use his money for the public good. The Anderson trustees bought the land adjacent to Hermann Hospital and created the Medical Center.*

Bottom: *Oilman J.S. Cullinan donated the land the Museum of Fine Arts stands on. The tract is a triangle at the junction of South Main and Montrose. Cullinan bought the site from the George Hermann Estate.*

125

126

Opposite top: *Cullinan was buying some Hermann land in the same area for himself at the time, in 1917. He bought the property along the west side of Main between the museum site and the Rice campus. Cullinan developed the Shadyside subdivision on this land. It was the most exclusive subdivision Houston ever had. Cullinan never offered any of the big Shadyside lots for sale to the general public. He sold them only to relatives and friends and business associates. Several of the early oil millionaires built homes in Shadyside.*

Opposite bottom: *Ross Sterling never lived in Shadyside, but he was one of the early oil millionaires. He was one of the founders of the Humble Company in 1917 and he was*

Humble's first president. Sterling sold out his interests in Humble in 1925. He served one term as governor from 1931 to 1933 and later founded the Sterling Oil Company.

Top: *Sterling built an extravagant summer house on Galveston Bay at LaPorte. The story is that he told the architect to build him a copy of the White House. The Sterling place is a little smaller than the White House, but some of the features are very similar. Governor Sterling left the estate to the Optimists' Club to be used as a home for boys. It was used for that purpose for a number of years; then banker Paul Barkley bought it and restored it. Barkley is dead now and the old mansion is for sale again.*

Someone also started a rumor that a white mob was marching toward the base. Neither report was true, but about 100 black troopers marched out of the base that night looking for revenge. Some whites armed themselves and went looking for the soldiers. Five policemen and 12 soldiers and civilians were killed. Another 24 people were wounded. Houstonians wanted to lynch the black soldiers. Mayor D.M. Moody got control of the situation by getting a declaration of martial law and a force of Coast Guardsmen from Galveston and soldiers from San Antonio to patrol the city.

The Army court-martialed 82 black soldiers. Thirteen were hanged. The others were sentenced to death or life in prison, but most were eventually released.

Houston and the rest of the country were caught up in the great experiment with Prohibition as the 1920s began. The Gulf Coast was well suited to rumrunning and there was never any shortage of intoxicants in Houston during the Prohibition era. Serious drinkers took precautions,

Opposite top: *The U.S. Army Air Corps developed a major training base south of Houston during World War I. Ellington Field came back to life in World War II. This is where the astronauts practice their flying and some National Guard jets are still based here. But most of the real estate is due to be turned over shortly to the city of Houston to become another civilian airport.*

Opposite bottom: *This photograph was made during World War I at Ellington. One of the student pilots and his instructor were about to take off for a night flight. It was a feat that required more nerve than skill.*

Above: *The Army stationed some black troops from the North at Camp Logan on the western edge of Houston in 1917. There was friction between the troops and the city's white police officers. Some of the black troops armed themselves, marched out of the base on the night of August 23 and started shooting at whites. Houstonians had been expecting trouble. Many of them were armed, too. They fired back. Seventeen people were killed.*

though, in case the new law turned out to be enforceable.

Howard R. Hughes invested some of the money he was making from his drill bits in booze. Noah Dietrich wrote in *Howard, The Amazing Mr. Hughes* that the senior Hughes bought all the stock of the Rice Hotel Bar when the bar closed June 25, 1918. The liquor was moved to the Hughes home on Yoakum and Howard, Jr., inherited what was left of it when his father died in 1924. Young Hughes left Noah Dietrich in charge of his Houston interests when he moved to Hollywood to make movies and discover new film stars. Dietrich says in his book that it became his duty to smuggle the Hughes booze to California. It was not illegal for Hughes to have the liquor for his own use, but it was illegal to move it from one place to another. Dietrich says he succeeded in shipping it in a railroad boxcar disguised as exposed movie film.

The 1920 Census placed the population of Houston at 138,276. The city was ranked number 45 in the nation that year. The population of the county was 186,667. Dallas and Bexar counties still had more people.

The city installed its first traffic signals in 1921. They were the kind featured in some of the Keystone Cops movies — metal "Stop" and "Go" signs that had to be operated by hand. George Fuermann of the *Houston Post* says Houston was the second city in the country to get these signals, after New York. The manual signals were replaced by automatic signals in 1927.

Will and Mike Hogg teamed up with Hugh Potter in 1923 to begin development of the tightly restricted River Oaks subdivision on a beautiful wooded tract on the western edge of the city.

The Hogg brothers about the same time sold to the city a large wooded tract on the north bank of Buffalo Bayou opposite their subdivision. This was the old Camp Logan site. The Hoggs bought the land when the Army turned it loose at the end of World War I. They sold it to the city at their cost but with a strict prohibition against its being used for anything except park purposes. This clause in the contract has caused the city to reject several propositions

*The house where Howard
Hughes, Jr. grew up is now part
of the campus of the University
of St. Thomas. The old Hughes
home is on Yoakum. The vault
where Howard Hughes, Sr. kept
his liquor during prohibition is
still in the basement.*

from drillers interested in prospecting for oil and gas in Memorial Park.

Two more cotton compresses were established on the ship channel by the early 1920s and the Anderson Clayton Company was beginning work on the Long Reach Terminal. Oil field equipment concerns were multiplying. Clarence Reed by this time had formed the Reed Roller Bit Company to manufacture a drill bit designed by Granville Humason. And H.S. Cameron's Iron Works in 1922 started manufacturing a blowout preventer designed by driller J.S. Abercrombie.

The ship channel was deepened to 30 feet in 1925. The port was ranked 11th in the nation in tonnage in 1926. The first grain elevator was established on the channel the same year. Eight refineries were operating on the channel by this time.

Natural gas was piped into Houston for the first time in 1926. It came from a field in Refugio. Only manufactured gas had been available before.

Opposite: *One of the original mansions in River Oaks is owned now by the Museum of Fine Arts. This home was built for Ima Hogg. She called it Bayou Bend. She filled it with rare antiques and lived here for many years before she gave the house and all the contents to the museum. Tour schedules can be obtained by calling 529-8773. Ima, Will and Mike Hogg were the children of James Stephen Hogg. He was the first native Texan to be elected governor. Hogg served in that office from 1891 to 1895. He made a fortune in oil and real estate after he left office.*

Above: *The River Oaks County Club is the centerpiece in the tightly restricted subdivision established in 1923 by Mike and Will Hogg and Hugh Potter. The clubhouse and many of the original homes have been expanded and updated as the value of the property here has increased.*

133

The Southern Motors Manufacturing Association made an automobile called the "Ranger Four" in Houston for about three years in the 20s. A company with a similar name had made a car called the "Dixie" here briefly, a few years earlier. Neither car made a hit with the motoring public.

Major new commercial buildings sprouted all over Houston during the building boom of the 20s. The Humble Company Building on Main was completed in 1921. This is

Opposite top: *Some of the original homes in River Oaks were fairly modest. The modest houses here are worth about $500,000 now. The mansions like this one John Staub designed for Hugh Roy and Lillie Cullen in 1933 are worth many millions. Hugh Roy Cullen was a member of a pioneer Texas family. He made a huge fortune in oil and gave most of it to the University of Houston and various hospitals. The Cullen home is occupied now by Oscar and Lynn Wyatt.*

Opposite bottom: *Less elegant but more famous is the River Oaks home of the late Dr. John Hill. He was a successful plastic surgeon and husband of the glamorous horsewoman Joan Robinson Hill. Joan died in 1969. Her rich father, Ash Robinson, blamed Dr. Hill. The*

doctor *was tried for murder in 1971, but a mistrial was declared. Dr. Hill was shot to death on the front porch of this home in 1972. Authorities considered it a hired killing. The alleged triggerman was killed before he could be tried. Two alleged go-betweens were convicted and sent to prison, but no one ever was charged with paying for the killing. The Gray Line includes the River Oaks area on one of its regular Houston bus tours. This is our Beverly Hills.*

Top: *The River Oaks Shopping Center on West Gray right outside the River Oaks gates was the first neighborhood shopping center in Houston. The center was looking very worn and tired until the Weingarten Realty Company restored it to its original condition in 1980.*

Opposite top: *There were many brands of automobiles in the early days of motoring. Two of the early cars were made in Houston. This is a four-cylinder Ranger produced by the Southern Motors Manufacturing Association in the mid-20s.*

Opposite center: *The Ford Motor Company assembled cars in a plant on Harrisburg from 1914 through 1942. The old Ford plant is now part of the Maxwell House Coffee division of General Foods. Maxwell House Coffee was produced originally by the Cheek and Neal Company of Nashville and Houston. Maryland Club Coffee was started by the Duncan Coffee Company of Houston. General Foods bought out Cheek and Neal in 1929. Coca Cola bought out Duncan in 1967.*

Opposite bottom: *The Humble Company did not go into retailing until the company was a couple of years old. The first Humble company service station in Houston was an ornate affair at the corner of Main and Jefferson. It was built in 1919 and demolished in 1982.*

Top: *The Merchandise Mart in Chicago was the inspiration for the Merchants' and Manufacturers' Building. This huge complex on North Main was built in the late 1920s to provide office and warehouse space for various kinds of businesses. It never caught on. The Depression was part of the problem, but merchants and manufacturers just didn't take to the idea. The building now houses the downtown branch of the University of Houston.*

137

the building now called the Main Building between Dallas and Polk. The Warwick Hotel and the city's Central Library Building were finished in 1926. The Neils Esperson Building was finished in 1927. Jesse Jones completed his Gulf Building in 1929. It was 35 stories tall and the tallest building in Houston until after World War II. But Jones was not devoted to tall buildings. He personally favored zoning laws and he thought downtown buildings should be limited to 10 stories. Other builders went above 10 stories, so Jones did, too. No one built anything taller than the Gulf Building until after Jones died. Respect for Jones may have had something to do with it. Anyone familiar with his views would have understood that any building he built was as tall as a building ought to be.

The Houston Buffs Baseball Stadium was completed in 1928. Dizzy and Daffy Dean both played there before they went on to stardom in St. Louis. Finger's Furniture Company now has a big store on the site where the stadium was and some Buff memorabilia is preserved in the Baseball Museum in the store.

A new concrete highway to Galveston was placed in service in 1928 and the first airmail plane landed at Ellington Field in February of that year.

The Democrats brought their 1928 convention to Houston because Jesse Jones promised to help with expenses and get a stadium built for the event. The stadium was built at Walker and Bagby where the Sam Houston Coliseum is today, within walking distance of Jones's Rice Hotel. Franklin D. Roosevelt came as a delegate from New

Above: *The Perfecto dry cleaning
plant on Fannin Street looks like
a church because the building
was a church originally. The
congregation of the Tuam
Avenue Baptist Church built it
in 1904. The congregation moved
to Main Street in 1920 and built
the South Main Baptist Church.
Perfecto bought this building
then and has occupied it
ever since.*

Right: *Ross Sterling was still
president of the Humble
Company when the company
built the first unit of the Humble
Building on Main Street between
Dallas and Polk. This building
changed hands and became the
Main Building when Humble
moved in the 1960s to the new
building on Bell, now called the
Exxon Building.*

Opposite: *George Hermann
wanted his money used for a
hospital that would provide free
medical care to the indigent. The
hospital the trustees of his estate
completed in 1925 provides some
free care to needy patients every
year. Hermann Hospital is also
a great, modern general hospital
— a teaching hospital for the
University of Texas Medical
School and a pioneer in
helicopter ambulance service.*

139

Opposite top: *Jesse Jones bought into the National Bank of Commerce shortly after it was founded. He eventually acquired controlling interest in the bank and by the late 1920s he was ready to move the bank into new quarters. He wanted something impressive. Jones contracted to build a new office building for Gulf Oil. He reserved space on the lower floors for the expanding Sakowitz specialty store and for his bank. The bank is now called Texas Commerce Bank and the banking lobby Jones built in 1929 is still the grandest one in town. The Texas Commerce holding company has since built a much taller building. Gulf Oil is moving to the new Gulf Tower in Houston Center. But the old Gulf Building on Main will continue to be the headquarters of the main unit of Texas Commerce Bank.*

Opposite bottom: *The trolley cars were gone from Main Street by the time the Gulf Building went up. Most of the overhead wires were gone, too. The parking meters had not appeared yet.*

Top right: *Clark Gable reputedly took acting lessons in this building in the 400 block of Hyde Park. The building was built in 1927 by drama coach and theatrical producer Frederick Leon Webster.*

Bottom right: *Cotton exports through the Port of Houston increased rapidly during the 1920s and Houston became the leading cotton port in the nation.*

York and nominated Al Smith for president. Young George R. Brown was there to help with some of the details. Roy Hofheinz was there as a page. But it was Jesse Jones's show.

Chairman Will Hogg and the City Planning Commission filed a report in 1929 recommending that Houston adopt a zoning ordinance, but most Houstonians were not interested.

The U.S. Navy accepted an invitation in 1930 to send the *USS Houston* here for a visit. The cruiser was the biggest ship to travel the ship channel up to that time. She stayed in Houston a week and Houstonians donated $15,000 to buy a silver service for the wardroom.

Houston had passed Galveston in size in 1910. The 1930 Census showed that Dallas and San Antonio had been passed, too. Houston's population was listed as 292,352. The city covered 72.2 square miles then. It was the biggest city in Texas and number 27 in the nation. There were 65 industrial plants on the ship channel and 475 manufacturing plants in the county. The channel was deepened to 32 feet in 1932 and to 34 feet in 1935. The rivalry between the ports of Houston and Galveston was still intense, but cotton farmers persuaded the two ports to equalize cotton rates in 1933.

The Port of Houston was ranked second in the nation in tonnage by 1930. There were 27 tanker lines serving the port, but the Depression, reduced foreign demand for U.S. grain, and a port strike all combined to reduce the port's business between 1930 and 1933. There was some gradual improvement after 1933, but the port's business did not

Opposite: *The Democrats held their 1928 national convention in a new stadium especially built for the purpose at Bagby and Walker in Houston. New York delegate Franklin D. Roosevelt nominated New York Governor Al Smith for the presidency. Smith lost to Herbert Hoover and Roosevelt was elected to Smith's old job as governor of New York.*

Top: *Houstonians entertained the crew and bought an elaborate silver service for the wardroom when the battlecruiser* USS Houston *visited the port in 1930. Any naval vessel visiting the city it was named for received the same treatment in those days.*

Right: *Only a couple of street names survive from the days when Texas had legal parimutuel betting and Houston had a horse track. There is a street named Epsom and a street named Downs but no trace of the stadium or the stables where Epsom Downs was (near the junction of the present U.S. 59 North Jensen Drive on the northeast side) in the mid-1930s.*

reach the level of 1930 again until 1939.

The Champion Paper Company built a big pulp mill on the ship channel in 1936 and didn't get the smell under control until many years later. The paper mill was the exception. The construction boom almost stopped until the WPA started work on the city hall, Lamar High School and the San Jacinto Monument. But Houston suffered less than most areas during the Depression. No banks failed. Jesse Jones got all the bankers together and arranged a system for the stronger banks to help the weaker banks stay afloat. Dime stores sold license plate frames imprinted with "Houston, Bright Spot of the Nation." Many people bought them and put them on their cars to spread the word. Bumper stickers had not yet been invented.

The first Houston Fat Stock Show and Rodeo was held in 1932 in the old Convention Hall built for the Democrats.

Mayor Oscar Holcombe ended the practice of having aldermen head the various city departments as a step toward making department heads responsible directly to

With fond memories

Lyndon B. Johnson

Opposite: *A young graduate of Southwest Texas State Teachers' College came to Houston in 1930 to teach public speaking at Sam Houston High School. Lyndon B. Johnson only stayed one year, but he coached the school's debate team to a state championship. He was 22 at the time. President Johnson signed this picture in the school's copy of the 1931 annual when he was here for a campaign speech in 1964.*

Top right: *Sam Houston High School now occupies a building on Irvington, built in the 1950s. The school was in the building pictured here when Johnson was teaching. This building was turned into an administration building for the district in the 1950s and then demolished when the present administration building on Richmond was built. The site is a parking lot now and the school district is offering it for sale at $12 million. It is the block bound by Capitol, Austin, Rusk and Caroline and it has a lot of history. The private Houston Academy opened on this site in 1859. The public school system acquired the site in 1880. The Houston High School was built on the site in 1895. It was later re-named Central High School and, when it burned, it was replaced in 1921 with the building shown here. This one was called Central High, too, until the name was changed to Sam Houston High in 1926.*

Bottom right: *Lyndon Johnson lived in a rented room in this house on Hawthorne when he was teaching school here in the 1930s.*

SAM HOUSTON HIGH SCHOOL

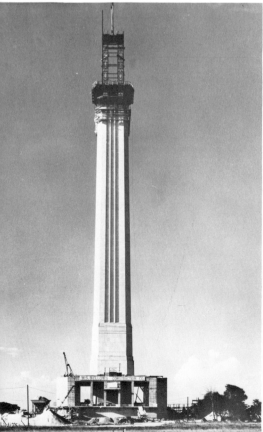

Above: *The first airline to fly passengers in and out of Houston was the now bankrupt Braniff Airways of Dallas. The year was 1935.*

Left: *Construction of the San Jacinto Monument began during the celebration of the 100th anniversary of the Battle of San Jacinto in 1936. The monument was designed by Alfred Finn of Houston. The federal government put up most of the money.*

Opposite: *The Burlington Line started running streamlined diesel trains between Houston and Dallas/Fort Worth in 1935. The service from Union Station was suspended about 30 years later for lack of passengers.*

the mayor. The wrangling over this helped to bring on a brief experiment with the city manager form of government during World War II.

Rain poured down on Harris County in 1935 and produced the worst flood Houston had experienced up to that time. Two-thirds of the county was under water. Several blocks of the downtown section flooded. This flood caused the Army Engineers to build the dams at Addicks and Barker to slow down the runoff from the rice fields north and west of the city.

The Burlington Rock Island put the Zephyr and the Rocket in service between Houston and Dallas/Fort Worth in 1935. The streamliners hit 90 and 100 miles per hour and covered the distance between Houston and Dallas in about four hours. Braniff started air service to Houston the same year and Eastern Airlines started a year later. The city bought the Houston Airport Corporation property on Telephone Road in 1937 and made it the Municipal Airport.

Howard Hughes won the International Harmon Trophy

in 1938 by flying around the world in three days, 19 hours and 14 minutes. He was invited to Houston to be honored with a parade. Hughes flew his plane in from Chicago. He was supposed to arrive at 11 a.m., July 30, but he got a favorable wind and was ahead of schedule. All three local radio stations were planning live coverage at 11. They would have to interrupt soap operas if the guest of honor arrived before that. One of the station managers got on the radio in the tower and tried to persuade the hero to do the honorable thing and delay his arrival. But other people's schedules never were very important to Hughes. He just flew on in early. The Houston City Council got carried away that day and named the airport for Hughes. The decision had to be rescinded when someone discovered a little later that city properties could not be named for living persons.

President Herbert Hoover named banker Jesse Jones to the Reconstruction Finance Corporation just before he left office in 1933. President Franklin D. Roosevelt made Jones chairman of the corporation. Jones was trusted by people who did not trust Roosevelt. He was the liason between the administration and business. He saved a lot of railroads, factories and banks from ruin. Jones was chairman of the RFC until 1939. He served as secretary of commerce and federal loan administrator for five years after that until he fell out with the Democrats and returned to Houston in 1945.

Rice graduate Albert Thomas was elected to Congress for the first time in 1936. He served until he died in 1966.

The Houston Independent School District established

Opposite top: *Howard Hughes was living in California in 1938 when he established a new record for flying around the world. He was agreeable when Houstonians suggested he should come back home long enough for a celebration in his honor.*

Opposite center: *The parade down Main Street drew more spectators than many recent parades have drawn. No one could have dreamed that day that the smiling hero would become a bitter recluse and eventually die of self-neglect on another flight to Houston in 1976.*

Opposite bottom: *All three of Houston's radio stations put the airport welcoming ceremonies on the air live.*

Bottom: *Jesse Jones went to Washington in 1933 to accept an appointment as a member of the National Reconstruction Finance Corporation. President Roosevelt later made Jones chairman of the commission. Jones also served as Roosevelt's secretary of commerce.*

Opposite top left: *Albert Thomas first came to Houston from Nacogdoches to attend the school then called Rice Institute. He was working as an assistant U.S. attorney here in 1936 when he decided to run for Congress. He was elected and he was reelected every two years after that until he died.*

Opposite top right: *This is the atrium in the University Center on the University of Houston Campus. Many of the buildings on the campus are named for* members of the Cullen family because Hugh Roy and Lillie Cullen gave the school so much money when it was a private institution. There was some sentiment at one time for naming the school Cullen. That didn't happen, but the street the campus fronts on was named Cullen.

Opposite bottom: *The University of Houston started as a junior college sponsored by the Houston Independent School District in 1935. The school moved to the present campus in 1939. It has been growing ever since. The university became a state school in 1963. Among the unique features of the University of Houston is the School of Hotel and Restaurant Management, endowed by the late Conrad Hilton.*

151

in 1935 the junior college that became the University of Houston. The first classes were held in temporary buildings on the campus of San Jacinto High School. The school moved to the present site in 1939 when Ben Taub and Julius Settegast donated the land.

M.D. Anderson of Anderson Clayton died in 1939, leaving $20 million for a foundation to benefit the public, advance knowledge and alleviate human suffering. His trustees gave some money to the University of Houston and to Rice, but they decided almost at the outset that the creation of a Texas Medical Center would be the Anderson Foundation's main business.

The Sam Houston Coliseum and Music Hall were completed in 1937. The monument at San Jacinto Battleground was completed in 1938. The new Houston City Hall was completed in 1939.

The 1940 Census credited Houston with a population of 384,514. That was 100,000 people more than were counted in Dallas that year. The population of the county was more than half a million. The population of the state topped six million for the first time.

Work started in 1941 on a new master street plan emphasizing thoroughfares and a loop system.

The old Ellington Field was reactivated in 1940 to train bomber pilots, navigators and bombardiers for the Army Air Corps. The Army also built a new training base for anti-aircraft units near Hitchcock in 1940 and named it Camp Wallace for Col. Elmer Wallace. He was an artillery officer killed in World War I in the Meuse-Argonne campaign.

Above: *The Baylor College of Medicine was so pleased to get an invitation to move from Dallas to Houston in 1943 that the school made the move before the Texas Medical Center could build the new building it promised. Baylor students attended classes during the first four years the medical school was in Houston in this warehouse building on what is now Allen Parkway.*

Right: *The present Houston City Hall was built by the WPA during the Depression. It was finished in 1939. The park area between the City Hall and Smith Street had been given to the city earlier by George Hermann. He wanted to be sure the city would have a place where people could sit down or take a nap if they wanted to. The block where the park and pool are today is where the Hermann family lived when George Hermann was a boy.*

Opposite: *The Houston Housing Authority tore down blocks of festering slums and the city's fanciest brothel in 1941 to build the low-rent housing project originally called San Felipe Courts. This project is now called Allen Parkway Village and it has become a slum.*

153

Camp Wallace was transferred to the Navy before the end of the war and the Navy closed it in 1946. The Navy also had a blimp base near Hitchcock during the time Navy blimps were conducting anti-submarine patrols over the Gulf. German submarines were sinking tankers in the Gulf; so the government built the Big Inch and Little Inch pipelines to carry liquid petroleum products from here to the Eastern seaboard. Texas Eastern Transmission Company bought the Big Inch and Little Inch lines after the war and converted them to carry natural gas as the Tennessee Gas Transmission Company's pipeline already was doing. Texas oil fields at the time were producing such a surplus of natural gas that most operators were simply flaring it in the fields. The highway between Houston and Galveston was illuminated at night by the flares in the oil fields along the way.

The war reduced the number of ships doing business at the Port of Houston and likewise at the Port of Galveston, but the big increase in demand for gasoline produced

Opposite: *The Southern Pacific Railroad was one of the biggest employers in town in 1910 when the railroad built this hospital for its employees. The Southern Pacific got out of the hospital business years ago and this building at 2015 Thomas Street is now part of the M.D. Anderson Hospital system. It is on the north bank of the bayou near* *downtown on land that will someday be about as valuable as any in town.*

Top: *Part of Memorial Park has been preserved in its natural state. Primitive trails wind through the Arboretum section of the park. Visitors should take plenty of insect repellant.*

expansion of the refineries along the Houston Ship Channel. New plants were built to make synthetic rubber. The Army took a big tract of channel-side property for an ordnance depot and built the Dickson Gun Plant on the north shore of the channel to make gun barrels. Hughes Tool Company managed the Dickson Plant until it closed in 1945. Two shipyards on the channel turned out small vessels for the Navy. Sheffield Steel built in 1942 the ship channel steel plant now known as Armco.

When the Japanese sank the cruiser *Houston* in 1942, Houstonians decided to replace it. A thousand volunteers were sworn in at a ceremony on Main Street to replace the crew. Houstonians bought $85 million worth of war bonds and the Navy gave the city's name to a warship already under construction. It became *USS Houston II*.

Voters approved a change in the form of the city government in 1942. Administrative responsibility was concentrated in a new office of city manager. There were eight city council members and a mayor. The mayor was the presiding officer of the council. He attended ceremonies and cut ribbons, but he did not run the government as Houston mayors had before. The plan was borrowed from Dallas and former Dallas city manager John North Edy was hired as the first city manager.

Plans were completed in 1945 for the Gulf Freeway between Houston and Galveston and the work started the following year.

The Texas Medical Center was conceived during the war years. The legislature set aside a half million dollars in

Opposite top: *People now come from all over the world to be treated at the Texas Medical Center. It is one of the most complete health-care complexes anywhere.*

Opposite bottom: *The M.D. Anderson Hospital Research and Tumor Institute started in the old Captain James A. Baker home on the near southwest side. It is housed now in a vast modern building faced with pink marble in the Texas Medical Center.*

1941 to start a cancer program. It was to be administered by the University of Texas. The trustees of the M.D. Anderson Foundation donated half a million dollars to the project. The University agreed to put the cancer institution in Houston and name it for M.D. Anderson.

Col. W.B. Bates and other Anderson trustees then proposed to establish a medical center south of Hermann Park adjacent to Hermann Hospital. Most of the land was owned by the city. The city had bought it from the George Hermann Estate with the idea of adding it to Hermann Park. Some prominent citizens objected to having the land used for anything but a park. So the city held an election. The voters approved the medical center plan. The M.D. Anderson Foundation bought the land from the city in 1944.

The Anderson Foundation had arranged with Baylor University in 1943 to move the Baylor College of Medicine from Dallas to Houston. The foundation offered a free building site and $1 million toward the cost of a building. The medical school moved to Houston before the building was built. Classes were held from 1943 until 1947 in a warehouse building that still stands at Waugh Drive and Allen Parkway. Allen Parkway was then a narrow, two-lane road called Buffalo Drive.

The Houston Chamber of Commerce raised $1 million in 1946 to help pay for the initial work on University of Texas institutions in the medical center and the building has been going on continuously ever since. ■

Opposite top: *Dr. Denton Cooley and his Texas Heart Institute are based at St. Luke's Hospital.*

Opposite center: *The Methodist Hospital in the Medical Center is where Dr. Michael DeBakey does his operating.*

Opposite bottom: *Some of the students studying at the Medical Center are housed in this old home facing Holcombe Boulevard on the bank of Brays Bayou. This was the home of the late mayor, Oscar Holcombe. His family donated the house to the Medical Center after Holcombe died in 1968.*

PART FOUR

Development Since World War II

"Houston is a city where few people think of anything but money . . . with a residential section mostly ugly and barren, a city without a single good restaurant . . ."
John Gunther, *Inside U.S.A.*, 1947.

"I prophesy that, within 50 years, Texas will lead all other states of the Union in population and wealth, that it will have the most economic and political power of any state and that Houston will be the fourth or fifth city in the United States in point of size."
Gen. Robert E. Wood, Chairman, Sears, 1951.

Everything built in Houston before World War II is dwarfed and overshadowed by what has been built since. The dominant buildings on the downtown skyline have been built in the last 15 years. Building permits issued in the five years preceeding World War II totalled $100 million. Permits for the year 1948 totalled $271 million. Some of the buildings built then already have been torn down to make way for bigger buildings.

Houston annexed another 142 square miles in 1948. This gave the city a total area of 216 square miles and an estimated population of 620,000. The city took in another 104 square miles in 1956 to make a total area of 320 square miles. This aggressive annexation policy has saved Houston from being hemmed in by separate municipalities as some other big cities have been.

The city had 33 passenger trains arriving and leaving every day in 1945. There were just 30 scheduled airplanes arriving and leaving each day, but the trend that would spell the end of the passenger train already had set in.

Work started on the tunnels under the ship channel in 1947. The Baytown Tunnel and the Washburn Tunnel at Pasadena both were completed in the early 1950s. The Washburn Tunnel was named for longtime Harris County auditor Harry Washburn.

The Navy built a big hospital on Holcombe Boulevard in 1946. It is now the VA Medical Center.

The University of St. Thomas was established in 1947 with headquarters in an old mansion at Montrose and West Alabama that was originally the home of developer J.W.

The Gulf Building (lower right) was the tallest building in Houston until after World War II. It is surrounded now by much taller buildings, with more to come.

Link and later the home of oil millionaire T.P. Lee.

A small group of theater enthusiasts started the Alley Theatre in a rented building on South Main the same year. Speech teacher Nina Vance was the director. Hugh Roy Cullen and his wife, Lillie, established their Cullen Foundation in 1947 and transferred to it assets worth an estimated $160 million to be used to help educational, medical and charitable institutions in the state of Texas. Cullen said they didn't want to wait until they were dead to give their money away because they enjoyed the giving of it. He enjoyed the attention their gifts brought him, too. He always made a speech.

Several new petrochemical plants were built on the ship channel during World War II. This trend continued during the years immediately after the war. Blue chip companies invested hundreds of millions of dollars in new plants to extract chemicals from the oil and gas being delivered to the channel area by dozens of pipelines. The channel was deepened to 36 feet.

Opposite left: *The demolishing company founded by Immanuel "Wrecker" Olshan in 1933 has been one of the chief beneficiaries of the prolonged Houston building boom. Olshan specializes in clearing away old buildings to make way for new buildings. This was the Atlanta Insurance Company Building at Louisiana and Prairie. A parking garage will take its place.*

Opposite top right: *Nina Vance was one of the founders and the first director of the Alley. She guided the theater until she died in 1980. The Alley won national recognition and built a splendid new building under her leadership.*

Opposite center right: *The famous Alley Theatre of Houston got that name because the entrance to the building where the theater started was through this alley off South Main Street. The theater was housed in an old fan factory off Smith Street for a number of years after it left here at the suggestion of the fire marshal.*

Opposite bottom: *J.W. Link developed the Montrose Addition. He built this mansion for himself at Montrose and West Alabama. It later was the home of the oil millionaire T.P. Lee. It has been the administration building for the University of St. Thomas since 1947.*

The big boom in air conditioning occurred during the five years following the end of the war. Houston became the most air-conditioned city in the world. Conventions had avoided Houston in the summertime before. Air conditioning made Houston a popular place for summertime conventions by the middle 50s.

Some experts claim that Houston never would have become an important city if it hadn't been for air conditioning. I don't believe this tells the whole story. Air conditioning certainly is a necessity here. Therefore, somebody in Houston would have invented it if somebody else had not. George Brown would have seen to it.

The Shamrock Hotel and the city's first television station both opened in 1949.

The Census of 1950 made Houston the 14th biggest city in America with a population of 596,163.

Houston was about as rigidly segregated as any city in the South at the end of World War II. The pattern of segregation had developed gradually over the years after the end of Reconstruction. The legislature adopted the poll tax and the politicians developed a system of white primaries to discourage blacks from voting. Many freed slaves had moved from the country into the cities after the Civil War because of false rumors that the Union was going to do something for them. Their descendants crowded into slums near downtown Houston.

Texas and the other states of the old Confederacy adopted a series of "Jim Crow" laws to keep the races separated. Railroads were required to furnish separate compartments and separate waiting rooms for blacks. Black people could occupy only certain seats on street cars and buses. School districts maintained separate schools for black children. All public buildings in Houston had separate restrooms and water fountains for blacks. No restaurant would serve blacks and whites in the same room. Black people were seldom seen in the Main Street stores.

The United States Supreme Court was still following the doctrine that separate schools were all right if they were reasonably equal when a black postal employee in Houston

Above: *The U.S. Navy turned the retired battleship* Texas *over to the state in 1948. The ship has been berthed at the San Jacinto Battleground ever since. It is open to visitors every day.*

Below: *The new Foley's department store opened in 1947 in a building covering the entire block bound by Main, Dallas, Travis and Lamar. Foley's had been bought a little earlier by the Federated department store chain. The original name was Foley Brothers and the old Foley Brothers building in the 400 block of Main became the home of the first Joske's store in Houston when Foley's moved to this new location.*

168

filed an application for admission to the University of Texas Law School in 1946. Heman Sweatt met all the requirements, but he was rejected because he was black. He filed a federal lawsuit, strongly supported by black publisher Carter Wesley. The state opposed the suit, but quickly established a law school for Negroes in Austin and created the Texas State University for Negroes out of what had been the Houston College for Negroes. This school later became Texas Southern University. The Supreme Court decided the separate schools were not equal and in 1950 the court ordered the UT Law School to admit qualified blacks. The court abandoned the separate-but-equal doctrine altogether in 1954 and banned all segregation on interstate trains and buses in 1955. "Colored" waiting rooms began to disappear.

The lawsuit that forced desegregation of the Houston public schools was filed in federal court in 1956. Two black students named Delores Ross and Beneva Williams asked to be admitted to the white schools near their homes. The

Opposite top: *Blacks were not admitted to the state universities in Texas before 1950 and there was no state university for black students until 1947. Blacks were beginning to go to court by then, seeking admission to the state universities. The legislature established Texas State University for Negroes in 1947. The name was later changed to Texas Southern University. There are no racial restrictions, but most of the students are black. The campus is on Wheeler Street a few blocks from the University of Houston Central Campus, where many black students are enrolled also.*

Opposite bottom left: *The Houston school board fought ideological battles from the mid-1950s until after 1970. The board changed superintendents several times as power shifted back and forth between liberals and conservatives. Billy Reagan has been superintendent of the Houston system now for eight years. He probably is one of the ablest school administrators in the country and he is pleased that the ideological contest has subsided so he can concentrate on improving the quality of education.*

Opposite bottom right: *The Houston school board was integrated long before the Houston school system was. Mrs. Charles White was elected to the board in 1958 while the board majority was using every device to delay desegregation of the public schools. Mrs. White served until 1967.*

court ordered the Houston school district to begin deseg-regating. The voters elected a black woman to the school board in 1958, but the board majority managed to delay complete desegregation of the schools until 1966.

Black students began staging sit-ins in coffee shops and lunchrooms during the 60s to force an end to segregation. The first place they visited was the lunch counter in the Weingarten's store on Almeda near the edge of a black neighborhood. They also visited Woolworth's, Walgreen's, Grant's and the City Hall Cafeteria. They usually were not served. The lunch counters were closed in most cases and the demonstrators were left sitting. The demonstrators followed a different plan when they moved the action to Main Street. They worked out in advance an arrangement with officials of Foley's department store that allowed several black students to be served at Foley's lunch counter. They were gone before news reporters heard about it. The ice was broken. The City Hall Cafeteria began serving blacks. Mayor Lewis Cutrer ordered an end to segregation at the city swimming pools in 1963. Mayor Roy Hofheinz had removed the "White" and "Colored" signs from the city hall in the early 1950s.

There were a couple of disturbances on the campus of Texas Southern University during this period in the middle 60s. Several dozen students started throwing things after a pep rally in November, 1965. Police closed off the area, questioned dozens of students and arrested four of them. One officer was wounded. The other disturbance in May, 1967, left several people injured. One police officer was killed, probably by a ricocheting bullet from another officer's gun. Four students were arrested.

Former mayor Oscar Holcombe ran for the office again in 1946, promising to do away with the city manager's office and restore the old "strong mayor" government. Houston-ians elected Holcombe and then approved the charter changes that increased his authority. Holcombe combined the powers of the city manager and the mayor in the one office. No mayor in America has more power than the mayor of Houston.

Holcombe served three two-year terms and was planning to run again in 1952, but his support dried up. Holcombe always had the backing of the Main Street establishment when he ran for mayor. The establishment consisted mostly of the rich and powerful men in the habit of meeting in Suite 8-F at the Lamar Hotel. They and Holcombe understood each other, but in 1952 the men in 8-F thought Holcombe stood a good chance of losing. The other major candidates were Councilman Louie Welch and

Mrs. Christia Adair was campaigning for Negro rights long before the civil rights movement was born. Mrs. Adair was born and raised in Edna. She came to Houston as a young woman and took up politics. She was Democratic chairman of the same black precinct for 25 years and she learned how to use her influence to help other blacks. Mrs. Adair is now 88. She is shown here discussing with Dr. John Biggers some sketches he has done for a mural. Dr. Biggers is professor of art at Texas Southern University. The Harris County Commissioners have commissioned him to execute a mural about Mrs. Adair's life for display in a new park named for her in the south end of the county.

former county judge Roy Hofheinz. The establishment preferred Hofheinz. He and Holcombe were so advised. Holcombe got out of the race and Hofheinz was elected.

Hofheinz had a brilliant mind and a forceful personality. He set out to remake Houston. He wanted more public works and more taxes to pay for them and he was soon in a hopeless deadlock with the more conservative city council. Council meetings were often interrupted by shouting and name calling. But Hofheinz was elected to another term. He and the council continued to disagree on the budget and nearly everything else. The council drew up 18 proposed amendments to the city charter to reduce the power of the mayor. Hofheinz forced another proposal onto the ballot. His amendment would move the city election date up one year. He made it plain that he hoped to get a new council elected.

The council drew up a set of impeachment charges and started holding hearings. Establishment lawyer Jack Binion stepped into Hofheinz's corner and outfoxed the council at every turn. Hofheinz was still in office on election day. The voters turned down all the amendments proposed by the council and approved only the Hofheinz proposal for a new election. A few people tried to tell Hofheinz that some of the voters might be anxious for a chance to vote for a new mayor, but he was sure the people wanted him and a new city council. He named a committee to pick a slate of council candidates and then went off on a trip to Europe. Hofheinz found when he returned that Oscar Holcombe was getting ready to run for mayor again. He didn't need anyone to explain to him that Holcombe had the support of the establishment. Holcombe wouldn't be running without it.

Hofheinz started a slashing attack on Holcombe and Jesse Jones and the Suite 8-F crowd. He said the voters had to choose between him and the "fat cats." He made some of the most abrasive campaign speeches ever made on Houston television. The medium was still new. Very few politicians had learned how to use it. Holcombe never did learn. Hofheinz told people the television camera was the greatest lie detector ever invented. He said no one could get away with lying to the camera. It was another way of saying that whatever he said on television must be true and he soon made it plain there was hardly anything he would not say on television. The voters learned more from Hofheinz's speeches that season than they had ever known before about who the main men in the establishment were — and they sided with the establishment. Six of the incumbent councilmen were reelected and Oscar Holcombe was elected mayor. Former councilman Louie Welch was returned to the council to continue his campaign for mayor. One of Hofheinz's former supporters in 8-F said, "Roy just got too big for his britches." Hofheinz departed from the city hall in a new Cadillac limousine he bought especially for the occasion.

A number of public works projects were carried out during the stormy three years of the Hofheinz administration. The Music Hall and Coliseum were remodelled. Work was started on the extension of Memorial Drive from

The area surrounding the city hall was occupied by parking lots, small business buildings and boarding houses during most of the years Oscar Holcombe was mayor. But Holcombe started thinking a long time ago about turning the area into a civic center. This has come to pass now and the city has named the center for the man Houstonians elected more often than anybody else to the office of mayor.

Opposite top: *The home that Will and Susan Clayton built in 1916 in the 5300 block of Caroline is now a branch of the Houston Public Library. The books and documents here deal exclusively with genealogy. Will Clayton was a partner in Anderson Clayton Company. He helped devise the Marshal Plan as undersecretary of state for economic affairs after World War II. The Clayton family donated the home to the library in 1958 after Will and Susan Clayton died.*

Opposite center: *The splendid old homes on Courtlandt Place are in demand again as more people realize the advantages of living close-in.*

Opposite bottom: *A similar street in the same area with the same appeal is Westmoreland Place. This house was moved to Westmoreland Place in 1905 from its original downtown location at Rusk and Caroline. The house was built in 1885.*

Below: *Montrose Boulevard is mostly commercial now, but Montrose once was a fine residential street. There was an esplanade down the middle of the boulevard with palm trees when Mr. and Mrs. W.W. Fondren built this mansion. Fondren was one of the founders of the Humble Company. The house is now a hotel and restaurant.*

Above: *The city of Houston built the terminal at what is now Hobby Airport in 1954. The commercial airlines all moved to the new Intercontinental Airport when it opened in 1969. Hobby handled only business and private planes for a few years. Then some commercial planes began using the old terminal. Now it is busier than ever. The city is enlarging the terminal building and putting up a new parking garage.*

Left: *The oldest educational television station in the United States is KUHT-TV, Channel 8, operated by the University of Houston.*

176

Shepherd into the city and on the Elysian Overpass. New restrictions were imposed on parking on downtown streets. Most downtown streets were converted to one-way and planning of the major thoroughfare system began. The new terminal at Houston International Airport (now Hobby) was completed in 1954. A proposal for a new airport was presented to the voters and rejected.

More corporations were moving their headquarters to Houston. Continental Oil established headquarters here in 1950. Prudential Insurance established a regional headquarters in the same year. Mobil, Gulf, Texaco, Tidewater Associated and Sunray Mid-Continent all expanded their Houston headquarters during the 1950s. The Ethyl Corporation opened a new $50 million plant on the ship channel in 1952.

The city was still relying entirely upon underground water. But the water table was dropping and the land was subsiding and it was increasingly plain that another source of water had to be found. Work started on Lake Houston on the San Jacinto River in 1952. The lake was completed in 1954 and the city began to deliver surface water to customers in the ship channel area.

The Gulf Freeway reached Galveston in 1953. It was one of the most advanced highways of the time, but the Texas Highway Department has been making improvements to it almost continuously ever since. The University of Houston put the first educational television station in the country on the air in 1953. KUHT-TV is now part of the Public Broadcasting System. It still occupies the building where it started. The building was built for ultra high frequency station KNUZ-TV. That station was years ahead of its time. It failed because hardly any Houston TV sets were equipped to receive UHF signals at the time.

Developer Frank Sharp announced plans in 1954 for the biggest subdivision in the country to be called Sharpstown. He projected 25,000 homes and a total investment of $400 million for the 6,500-acre development on the southwest side of town. Much of the land had previously been a dairy.

The Houston Chamber of Commerce calculated that the population of the greater Houston area would reach one million in July, 1954. The chamber appointed a committee to decide exactly which newcomer would be the one-millionth. The committee picked a Cities Service employee named Barney McCasland. He was given the title "Mr. Million" and a lot of gifts and led through a series of public relations exercises. McCasland was later transferred away as oil people so often are. But others kept coming.

A new produce terminal was completed off Old Spanish Trail in 1954 replacing the public market that had sprawled over several downtown city blocks northwest of the city hall.

The voters' failure to approve a new airport was a major worry for city officials. Developers were buying up vacant land in the county at such a rate that there was concern whether a big tract reasonably near the city could be had at a price the city could pay by the time the voters were willing. There was some discussion about this between

Opposite left: *The Houston Chamber of Commerce made a big fuss when Barney McCasland moved to Houston in 1954. The chamber reckoned that the population of Greater Houston reached one million when McCasland arrived. So McCasland was awarded some prizes and sent on a flying trip around the country to notify other cities of the Houston milestone. McCasland lives in Midland now, but he enjoyed being Mr. Million. He says he wouldn't mind living in Houston again.*

Opposite top: *The downtown block where Houston's earlier city halls stood is called Market Square to this day because it was the place farmers parked their wagons and sold the produce they brought to town in* the early days. Shops were included in the last two city hall buildings to occupy the site. The city built a large produce market nearby when the city government moved to the present city hall in the 1930s. Most of the area between Market Square and the bayou was occupied by grocery and produce dealers until the 50s.

Opposite bottom: *Now the big dealers have their headquarters on Produce Row off Old Spanish Trail, but some farmers bring their produce to the Farmers' Cooperative Market on Airline Drive. Many thrifty Houston housewives do their marketing here.*

Mayor Holcombe after he returned to office and the wealthy men in Suite 8-F. The upshot was that some of the wealthy citizens formed a syndicate and started buying up land in north Harris County without letting the sellers know what was up. They had an understanding with the mayor that the land would be offered to the city at the same price they paid when the city was ready to move. There was no public announcement of this at the time, of course.

There were 475,000 motor vehicles registered in Harris County by 1955 and 8,000 of them were air-conditioned. Neiman-Marcus came to Houston that year. The Dallas company bought out Ben Wolfman's Fashion in the Kirby Building on Main Street. The store in the Kirby Building was closed when Neiman's opened the Galleria store in 1969. All the other major Main Street retailers have moved to the suburbs now, but Foley's and Sakowitz still maintain large stores on Main Street in addition to their suburban outlets.

The Houston Grand Opera was established in 1955.

Opposite top: *Houstonians less concerned about thrift buy their produce at Jim Jamail and Sons on Kirby Drive. Jim Jamail was an immigrant from Lebanon. He had a little fruit stand on Market Square, where he sold nothing but the best produce obtainable. Jamail and his three sons opened a grocery store on Montrose after World War II. The sons moved the business to Kirby Drive after Jim Jamail died. Joe and Albert bought out their brother, Harry. Now Albert, on the right, has bought out Joe and he is the head of the firm. Jamail's still does business the same way Jim Jamail did — no sales, no specials, just the best food that can be had and, probably, the only 5-cent Coca Cola machine in Houston.*

Opposite center left: *The produce and grocery merchants have left Market Square now, but a few old-timers are still in the area. There was a movement in the 60s to preserve the little 18th-century buildings around the square. Night clubs and restaurants blossomed in the old buildings, but the good times didn't last. Most of those businesses are gone now. Still surviving is La Carafe Bar in the oldest commercial building in town on Congress between Milam and Travis.*

Opposite center right: *This little building was once a stage station. It has a tiny brick patio at the back.*

Opposite bottom: *Leo Stelzig still sells Western gear on Preston just off the old square. His grandfather founded this business. It has been at this location since 1926.*

Houston voters in 1956 approved a plan to expand the port and buy the Long Reach docks from Anderson Clayton Company. Jesse Jones died in 1956, leaving most of his fortune to a charitable foundation he called Houston Endowment, Incorporated. Jones owned or controlled 49 buildings when he died.

The Gulfgate Shopping Center opened in 1956 with David Daum as manager. Gulfgate was the first big regional shopping center in Houston. It was built around an open

Opposite top left: *Shudde Brothers store was at Travis and Preston on the square until the owner tore the building down and put in a parking lot in the 1970s. Weldon Shudde (left) moved the retail hat business then to the old Shudde Brothers hat factory building at 905 Trinity. Shudde's has specialized in cleaning and blocking hats here for generations. John Wayne used to send all his dirty hats here.*

Opposite center left: *Henry Henke came to Houston from New Orleans in 1872. He started a store and in 1882 he hired C.G. Pillot to work for him. Pillot was a good worker; so Henke made him a partner. They turned Henke's store into the first major grocery chain in Houston. Henke and Pillot was bought out by Kroger's in the 1960s. Henry Henke built this building at Congress and Milam on Market Square in 1924. A new owner modernized it in 1982. The original building on this site was Pamelia Mann's Mansion House Hotel.*

Opposite bottom left: *Several of the old buildings around Market Square have been torn down since the revival fizzled out. One of the survivors is this little building at 316 Milam Street. It was built by John Lang probably about 1896. Downtown historian Ann Wilson says it was Victorian originally and the New Orleans embellishments were added when a restaurant opened here in the 1960s.*

Opposite top right: *The building at 800 Commerce had been a warehouse and the home of several commercial enterprises before a law firm bought it in the late 1970s and turned it into an elegant office building.*

Opposite bottom right: *This old fragment of the Magnolia Brewery and Ice Company, around the corner on Milam, is still waiting for some architect to discover some merit in it.*

mall. The mall was not covered and air-conditioned until later.

The Texas Highway Department settled on a new route for U.S. Highway 59 South in 1957. The decision was a major victory for developer Frank Sharp. The highway was being developed into a major freeway. Sharp wanted to make sure it would pass through his Sharpstown subdivision. He persuaded other landowners in the area to join him in offering to donate the right of way. The offer was accepted. Sharp and the others donated land worth more than $2 million and they all wound up with valuable freeway frontage. Sharp laid out a huge shopping center alongside the freeway in Sharpstown.

The Royal Dutch Airline, KLM, started service between Houston and Amsterdam in 1957. Harris County established a new park commission in 1958 to look into building a new stadium to accommodate the stock show. Some hoped such a stadium might attract a major league ball club to Houston.

The ship channel was deepened to 40 feet in 1958 and Congressman Albert Thomas persuaded the Army to give up the San Jacinto Ordnance Depot to make room for more industries on the channel.

Jet planes began flying regularly from Houston International that year and the Harris County Heritage Society completed the restoration of the 1847 Kellum-Noble House in Sam Houston Park.

The Humble Company announced plans in the late 50s for a new headquarters building on Bell. It would be 44

Opposite: *This may be the oldest house in Harris County still standing on its original site. It surely is the oldest brick house in the county. Nathaniel Kellum built this house in 1847 on what was then the western edge of the city. The city bought the house and land in the 1890s for what became Sam Houston Park. The house was headquarters for the Park Department for a time and later it was used as a place to store equipment and junk. It was in bad shape in 1954 when the Harris County Heritage Society was organized to save it. The society completed restoration of the Kellum House in 1958 and since then has restored and moved to the park several other valuable old buildings.*

Above right: *This building has changed names twice since it was built in 1960. The oil company that built it was called the Humble Company when the work started. The company later changed its name to Enco. Now the company is Exxon, USA and this is the Exxon Building. The Petroleum Club occupies the top two floors. There was an observation deck open to the public when the building was new, but the observation deck has been closed. A building of 44 floors no longer seems that high.*

Right: *The first big regional shopping center in Houston was Gulfgate on the Gulf Freeway at the South Loop. Newcomers claim that Houstonians call this place "Guffgate."*

Top: *The American General Center is being developed on Allen Parkway between Montrose and Waugh Drive by the insurance company the late Gus Wortham founded in 1926. Hedy Lamarr once lived on the site where the tallest building is rising. This site at Waugh and Allen Parkway was occupied in the 1950s by the Buffalo Townhouses. The townhouses were owned by the Lee Brothers Oil Company. Howard Lee and Hedy Lamarr lived in one of the townhouses briefly after they married and before they moved into a home in River Oaks.*

Center: *Gus Wortham began acquiring the property where the American General Center is before 1930. He also bought part of the old Magnolia Cemetery next door to the center. Wortham directed that a mausoleum be built to hold his remains and those of his wife, Lyndall. He was interred here when he died in 1976 and she in 1980. Wortham told some of his associates he wanted to be where he could keep an eye on things. All the buildings in the American General Center are visible from the mausoleum.*

Bottom: *Construction of Houston Intercontinental Airport took months longer than scheduled and the contractor went bankrupt. But it has worked about as well as any other modern airport.*

stories, the tallest building in the South for a brief time. K.S. "Bud" Adams got an American Football League franchise in 1959. His Houston Oilers played their first games in Jeppeson Stadium. It was a high school stadium at the time. It is now the University of Houston practice field. The name has been changed to Robertson Stadium.

The 1960 Census made Houston the sixth largest city in the United States with a population of 938,219. The building boom continued in the downtown area. The Humble Building, Cullen Center, the First City National Bank Building, the Sheraton-Lincoln Hotel and office building, the World Trade Center and the new Federal Office Building and Post Office all were under construction. Fourteen major new office buildings were completed in the downtown area between 1960 and 1969. In the same period, in the suburbs, Gerald Hines began building the Galleria complex, Kenneth Schnitzer started Greenway Plaza and the American General Company built the first building in the American General Center on Allen Parkway at Waugh. Tall buildings were no longer confined to downtown and South Main Street.

Rice Institute changed its name to Rice University in 1960 and, four years later, the school obtained court permission to disregard some provisions of William Marsh Rice's will. Rice had specified that his school was to provide free education to white students. A court ruling in 1964 lifted the racial restriction and permitted the school to begin charging tuition.

Mayor Lewis Cutrer and the city council accepted the proposed new airport site in north Harris County and paid the syndicate the price the syndicate had paid — $1,980,463 for 3,126 acres. There was official praise for the generosity and far-sightedness of the syndicate members. If land they bought on their own account in the same area appreciated because of the airport, nobody was inclined to complain about it. It was the Houston way of doing things. Work started in 1962 on what came to be called Houston Intercontinental Airport. The name strikes some travelers as pretentious since every other city is satisfied to have an

international airport, but Houstonians are not embarrassed about having the only intercontinental airport.

The old city hall building on Market Square burned in 1960. The city had rented the building out after the new city hall was built in 1936. Part of the old place was being used as a bus terminal when the fire occurred. Some downtown interests pressed the city to sell the site for commercial development, but the city council decided to keep it as a park.

Congressman Albert Thomas learned in 1961 that the National Aeronautics and Space Administration was shopping for a site for the Manned Spacecraft Center. Thomas steered the NASA people to Harris County. The Humble Company owned 30,000 acres of land on the north shore of Clear Lake. Humble gave 1,000 acres of this land to Rice University and Rice offered it to the space agency. NASA announced in September that the Manned Spacecraft Center would be built on the land donated by Rice University. Congressman Thomas said most of the credit was due President John Kennedy, Vice President Lyndon Johnson, Humble Company Board Chairman Morgan Davis and Rice University Board Chairman George R. Brown. George Brown always said Albert Thomas played the key role. Thomas was chairman of the House subcommittee that controlled NASA's money. Brown's company got the contract to build the Manned Spacecraft Center. The Humble Company developed Clear Lake City on part of the land the company still owned near the Space Center.

The first completely air-conditioned shopping mall in

Opposite: *All of the space base and all of Clear Lake City too are on land that once was the private domain of Jim West. He made a fortune in lumber and land and he built this handsome house on his vast ranch on the north shore of Clear Lake. The Humble Oil Company bought this ranch in the 1930s and gave part of it to Rice University so Rice could give it to NASA. The old house is now a kind of "think tank" for space scientists.*

Top right: *No spaceship ever has been launched from the Lyndon B. Johnson Manned Spacecraft Center at Clear Lake, but there is an assortment of spaceships and rockets on display at the base. The base is a major tourist attraction and the tourists expect to see some rockets.*

Center: *There are elaborate displays of space hardware indoors as well as out and visitors are seldom disappointed. All the launchings take place in Florida. The base here does the planning and controls the flights. Visitors are sometimes allowed in the Mission Control Center. They can also visit the base cafeteria, where they may occasionally see an astronaut.*

Bottom: *Developer Frank Sharp completed the first fully air-conditioned shopping mall in Houston in 1961. His Sharpstown State Bank occupied the dark glass building at the right.*

the city opened in 1961. It was Sharpstown Center on the Southwest Freeway at Bellaire Boulevard.

Houston escaped with relatively minor damage when Hurricane Carla came ashore in September, 1961. The great storm caused $330 million damage in the coastal area between Port Arthur and Corpus Christi.

County voters approved a revenue bond issue in 1961 to finance the proposed new county stadium. Some baseball fans including Craig Cullinan, Jr., and George Kirksey formed a corporation to go after a major league baseball franchise. Cullinan and Kirksey invited R.E. "Bob" Smith and Roy Hofheinz to join them in the baseball venture. Smith was a very wealthy oilman and strong supporter of Hofheinz when Hofheinz was mayor. Hofheinz was widely believed to be capable of selling anything to anybody. The original corporation was soon reorganized as the Houston Sports Association with Smith and Hofheinz as the principal stockholders. Hofheinz decided that any new county stadium would have to be covered and air-conditioned. He had a team of architects and engineers start work on the concept. He took a model of the concept to a meeting of the National League owners in Chicago and he came back with a franchise. The Houston Sports Association then bought out the Houston Buffs' American League franchise. The team's name was changed to Colt .45s and Houston began playing in the National League in 1962. The covered stadium was still just an idea. The Colts played their home games in a temporary stadium.

The county held a new stadium bond election and the voters approved $22 million in bonds supported by tax revenues for a new stadium. The revenue bonds approved at the previous election never were sold. The county picked a site for the stadium off South Main Street on the proposed South Loop. Excavation began in December, 1961. The contractor had a hole in the ground 700 feet across and 24 feet deep by May, 1962, when it became apparent that the money was going to run out before the stadium was finished. The county commissioners went back to the voters with a proposal for another $9.5 million.

Top: *The Astrodome is nearly 20 years old now and showing some wear. The roof has been done over and the upholstery needs to be. But the original covered air-conditioned stadium still draws crowds of tourists for the guided tours between games.*

Above: *The Astrodome is far more then a sports stadium. The mammoth National Homebuilders conventions have been held here several times and the Offshore Technology Conference meets nowhere but here. The OTC is the biggest business conference in the world, bringing together the makers and the users of offshore oil equipment.*

Hofheinz used all his persuasive powers and the second bond issue was approved. Hofheinz and Smith were looking for a new name for the ball team by 1964 because of problems with the Colt firearms people. Hofheinz decided the team would be the Astros and the stadium would be the Astrodome. Mickey Herskowitz complained that Astros was a name sports writers would not find easy to shorten for headlines. It took them a while, but eventually they settled on "Stros." The county owns the Astrodome. The Houston Sports Association has a long-term lease and control over the entire plant.

Marcella D. Perry became president of the Heights Savings Association in 1962, succeeding her father, James G. Donovan. He and she founded the association in 1954.

Air France began service to Paris from Houston International Airport in 1962. And the bus company went into receivership.

The first section of the West Loop was opened to traffic in 1963. It was the section between Memorial Drive and the Southwest Freeway, now the most congested and dangerous thoroughfare in Texas.

The new Ben Taub Hospital opened in the Texas Medical Center in 1963. This hospital and the older Jeff Davis Hospital were operated jointly by the city and county for people unable to afford private hospital care. The arrangement was not a harmonious one. The city and county argued constantly over the budget. The hospitals were often in danger of running out of money. A proposal to create a hospital district to collect a tax and operate the charity hospitals was rejected by the county's voters four times before Ben Taub was built. Dutch playwright Jan de Hartog was teaching in Houston at the time. He is a humanitarian and a Quaker. He volunteered to work as an orderly at Ben Taub. The playwright was shocked at the conditions. He wrote newspaper articles and a book about his experiences. These probably helped generate the favorable vote on the hospital district question the fifth time it came up in 1965.

The University of Houston was taken into the state

Top: *Donald Bonham and O.C. Mendenhall took over an old Kroger's supermarket on Fulton Street in the early 1970s and established a supermarket with a Spanish accent. Their Fiesta Mart was a big success and they now have nine other stores in various parts of the city. It is the classic success formula. They found something no one else was doing and they are doing it.*

Center: *Ninfa Laurenzo was a widow with no capital when she started serving Tex-Mex food in this small place on Navigation a few years ago. Downtown workers started eating lunch here and they spread the word about Ninfa's tacos. The place was soon drawing capacity crowds. Ninfa now has restaurants in several Houston suburbs and in several other cities.*

Bottom: *The private airport Charlie and Irma Hooks established on Steubner-Airline Road in northwest Harris County in 1963 is now the biggest privately owned airport in the United States. Charlie and Irma named the airport for their son, David Wayne Hooks, after he was killed in a plane crash in 1965.*

Opposite top left: *The Gulf Coast Railroad Association maintains a small railroad museum on Mesa Drive. It is open to visitors only on Sundays between 10 am and 4:30 pm. Serious railroad buffs will also want to visit the much more elaborate museum in the old Santa Fe building in Galveston.*

Opposite top right: *Some people wonder when they pass the A.J. Foyt Chevrolet Agency on South Post Oak Road whether the champion race driver actually spends any time in the showroom. He does. Foyt says anything that has his name on it, he runs.*

Opposite center left: *The old town of Spring has many new residents. They have tried to preserve some of the past by building a cluster of antique stores and shops around this ancient store building. Spring is just off I-45 North. The Hanna-Barbera Company has announced plans for a big new theme park near here.*

Opposite center right: *The new Herman Brown Park on the northeast side was donated to the city in 1979 by the Brown Foundation. It is named for the late Herman Brown of Brown and Root. Access is by Mercury Road off I-10 East.*

Opposite bottom: *The most striking examples of white flight and blockbusting in Houston occurred in the 1960s in the Riverside Terrace area. The fine homes on the streets north and south of Brays Bayou here were occupied mostly by whites. The establishment of Texas Southern University nearby helped to bring black families into the area. Many of the whites fled and sold their homes at bargain prices. The area is occupied now largely by affluent blacks and the prices of homes are high and rising.*

Top: *The Miller Memorial Theater in Hermann Park was originally just a stage with open-air seating. The section of permanent seats and the partial roof were added later. The original stage was built in the 1920s with $50,000 the late Jesse Miller left for that purpose.*

Top: *The building Gerald Hines built for the Shell Oil Company is on the right in this picture, facing the city hall. It is 50 stories. The dark building on the left is Pennzoil Place. The building between Pennzoil Place and the Shell Building is the light company's building. The building behind Pennzoil Place is the Texas Commerce Tower. It is 75 stories and the tallest building in town, for the moment.*

Center: *Roy Hofheinz and others interested in the Astrodome argued in the 1960s against the building of any more convention buildings. They said there would not be enough convention business to go around, but the city built a big new convention hall in the downtown civic center anyway. This hall is named for the late Congressman Albert Thomas. City officials already are talking about building a bigger center.*

Bottom: *The Albert Thomas Convention Center was designed so as not to disturb this big oak tree. This is the Courthouse Oak, also called the Hanging Oak. The county's criminal courthouse stood behind this tree for about 70 years. There are stories about criminals being hanged from the tree, but they probably are not true.*

Opposite: *A towering lobby with a glass roof is the only connection between the two glass towers of the unique Pennzoil Place, designed by Philip Johnson.*

university system in 1963. The Baptist General Convention established Houston Baptist College in Sharpstown the same year. The school is now called Houston Baptist University. It occupies a valuable tract of land donated by developer Frank Sharp. Sharp also donated land for two Catholic schools in the early days when he was trying to make sure the freeway came his way.

Mayor Louie Welch signed an agreement in 1964 for another source of surface water for the city. The agreement with the Trinity River Authority provided for the development of Lake Livingston. Work started in 1965. The lake was finished in 1969.

Two high-rise apartment buildings were built in downtown Houston in 1965. They were largely ignored and there has not been an apartment house built downtown since.

U.S. Steel announced plans in 1965 for a big mill at Baytown.

Roy Hofheinz and Bob Smith fell out. Smith challenged Hofheinz to buy him out. He thought Hofheinz could not raise the money, but Hofheinz did. He bought most of Smith's stock and became the master of the Astrodome operation.

The city started work on the Albert Thomas Convention Center downtown in 1966. The Jesse H. Jones Hall for the Performing Arts opened as the new home of the Houston Symphony, the Houston Grand Opera and the Houston Ballet. Developer Gerald D. Hines and the Shell Oil Company announced plans for a new building for Shell. The original plan called for 47 stories, but the builders went on up to 50

floors and Number One Shell Plaza was the tallest building in town, briefly.

Air pollution provoked a showdown between the Houston City Hall and the ship channel industries in 1967. The ship channel never had been annexed to the city. The absence of city taxes and city regulations was one of the incentives that drew industry to the channel. Mayor Louie Welch put the industries on notice that they might be annexed to the city if that was what it took to get pollution under control. This threat brought on a series of negotiations and a compromise. The channel plants were allowed to sign agreements with the city making them industrial districts, subject to some city controls, and requiring them to pay some money to the city in lieu of taxes. If they didn't sign, they would be annexed. Only one property owner refused to sign.

The Hofheinz family opened Astroworld Park in 1967.

The new Alley Theatre opened in the downtown Civic Center in 1968.

The Houston Oilers started playing their home games in the Astrodome in 1968 after Roy Hofheinz and Bud Adams finally agreed on the rent.

The National Association of Homebuilders held its annual convention in the Astrodome complex in 1969. It was the biggest convention yet for Houston and the first time the homebuilders had met outside Chicago.

Shell Oil announced in 1969 that it would move a substantial part of its headquarters operation from New York to the new Shell Building in Houston.

Opposite: *Nina Vance moved the Alley Theatre from the old fan factory to a conspicuous new location in the downtown civic center in 1968. The late Jesse Jones's Houston Endowment, Incorporated, donated the site. The Ford Foundation provided part of the money for this building. The name was changed to Nina Vance Alley Theatre after Nina Vance died. Iris Siff took over direction of the theater then. She was murdered by a burglar in her office here early in 1982.*

Top right: *Roy Hofheinz personally planned and built the Astroworld Park across the South Loop from the Astrodome. He eventually lost control of the park and all the rest of his Astrodomain empire because of overwhelming debt. Astroworld is operated now by the Six Flags Company.*

Center: *Dr. Denton Cooley performed the first American heart transplant operation at St. Luke's Hospital in 1968. He did 20 more transplants over the next 18 months. He stopped because so many of his patients rejected their new hearts. Dr. Cooley and his associates at the Texas Heart Institute began doing transplants again in 1982 with a new drug that promised to prevent rejection. Cooley is a native Houstonian. He played basketball at the University of Texas at Austin.*

Bottom: *Retailers began leaving downtown in the late 1960s. Neiman-Marcus moved from Main Street to this new building in the Galleria.*

The Houston Intercontinental Airport opened in June of 1969. And the spaceship *Eagle* reported to Houston on July 20 that it had landed on the moon.

The Census of 1970 showed a population of 1,232,802 — almost double the 1950 population.

Developer Gerald D. Hines opened his Galleria Shopping Center at the intersection of Westheimer Road and South Post Oak in 1970. Sakowitz and Joske's already had built large stores at the same intersection, where there had been only a country store and a country school house a few years before. The Galleria complex has helped attract other businesses to what developers call the "Magic Circle." The concentration of office towers, commercial buildings and hotels is greater at this location now than anywhere else except downtown.

Downtown development continued at a fast pace in the 1970s. One Shell Plaza and Two Shell Plaza were completed in 1971 and in the same year two new projects were initiated, both of them bigger than anything ever done

Opposite bottom: *A concentration of office buildings, hotels and shops has grown up in one generation around what was the intersection of two country roads. This is what the intersection of Westheimer and Post Oak looked like from the air in the middle 1950s. There was a country school house where Neiman's is now and a country store on the corner where Joske's is now.*

Top: *The Galleria was what really got the Westheimer-Post Oak boom started, but Sakowitz had built a big store 10 years earlier on the northwest corner of the intersection. Joske's built on the southeast corner of the magic intersection in 1963.*

Center: *A trend toward large downtown developments, spreading over several blocks actually started with Cullen Center and continued into the 1970s. Work started in 1971 on Allen Center on 18 acres bound by Dallas, Louisiana, Bell and I-45.*

Bottom right: *Most of the land Allen Center occupies was formerly part of the Fourth Ward black ghetto. The developers did their best to get possession of the old Antioch Baptist Church, but the black congregation refused to sell. So Allen Center is being built around the little church.*

Top: *Allen Center and Cullen Center will meet when this construction is finished. The Four Allen Center Building, on the south end of Allen Center, will stand next door to the 1600 Smith Building at the north end of Cullen Center.*

Center: *Texas Eastern Transmission Company and Cadillac-Fairview are building Houston Center on 33 blocks of land east of Main Street.*

Bottom left: *The Houston Center features walkways over the streets. Escalators connect the buildings with the growing underground pedestrian tunnel system.*

Opposite right: *It is possible to walk from Houston Center on the east side to Allen Center on the west side without leaving the tunnel system. The small shops and cafes in the tunnels seem to be doing well and they will do much better if people ever start living downtown. The Houston Center developers say they plan some residential buildings eventually. The new Four Seasons Hotel in Houston Center has more than 100 apartments for permanent residents.*

Opposite far right: *Camille Berman grew tired of waiting for something to happen to keep downtown alive after dark. Berman is the owner of Maxim's Restaurant. Tony's gets more press and a flashier crowd, but Maxim's is the original fancy restaurant in Houston. It was downtown for 33 years before Berman moved it to Greenway Plaza in 1982. He says his lunch business in not as good here, but the dinner business is much better.*

downtown before. Trammell Crow and the Metropolitan Life Insurance Company started work on Allen Center on an 18-acre site between Smith Street and Interstate 45 just south of the Civic Center. A big part of this property had been part of the old Fourth Ward slum until the building of the elevated freeway cut it off from the main body of Fourth Ward. Texas Eastern Transmission Company bought up 33 blocks east of Main Street for a development called Houston Center, emphasizing advanced design, elevated walkways and landscaped spaces. Houston Center is supposed to have 23 million square feet of offices, hotels, stores, shops and apartments eventually. Some developers still believe that some Houstonians one day will want to live downtown.

Construction began in 1970 on Lake Conroe on the West Fork of the San Jacinto River, another addition to Houston's water supply.

Shell Oil bought 500 acres of land near the Astrodome and started a new commercial and residential develop-

204

Opposite top left: *The disciples of zoning claim that Greenway Plaza is an example of what Houston could be with zoning. All the buildings, all the open spaces and all the landscaping here were planned by the same planners.*

Opposite top right: *It hasn't happened yet, but the Italian developer of this condominium tower in the Galleria area thinks foreigners are going to buy many of the apartments in this building and the one just like it that he has built next door. This building and its twin are the Four Leaf Towers.*

Opposite bottom left: *A spider spinning a web has captured the attention of this visitor in the Armand Bayou Park. The park is a wilderness preserved next door to the University of Houston Clear Lake Campus. The entrance is on Bay Area Boulevard. The park was named for the late Armand Yramategue. He was curator of the Burke Baker Planetarium and president of the Texas Conservation Council when he was murdered by robbers in 1970.*

Opposite bottom right: *Armand Bayou is a favorite with canoeists. They can put their canoes in the water at the county's Bay Area Park on Bay Area Boulevard. No power boats are allowed here. There are free boat tours four times a day. The phone number for reservations is 221-6126.*

Top: *All the tall buildings in Houston are not office buildings and apartments. These at Studemont and Washington are storage bins for rice. Texas produces much of the U.S. rice crop. Most of the American rice crop is exported and much of the Texas crop passes through here. American Rice, Incorporated, is the biggest rice mill on the Gulf Coast. The first building here was built in 1902 by Standard Milling Company. The plant was enlarged several times and it changed hands several times before ARI bought it from Blue Ribbon Mills in 1975. ARI still produces the Blue Ribbon brand rice here.*

ment called Plaza del Oro.

Work started on the Eleven Hundred Milam Building, taller than anything else in Houston except One Shell Plaza.

Memorial Hospital decided to sell its downtown property and build a new hospital in Sharpstown. Classes began in the new University of Texas Medical School in the Medical Center and the Houston Fire Department took over the operation of emergency ambulances in the city in 1971. Most of the ambulances in Houston previously had been operated by undertakers. Some of them deplored the change as a blow to private enterprise.

The U.S. Steel Plant at Cedar Point in Baytown was completed in 1971.

The Securities Exchange Commission filed suit that same year accusing developer Frank Sharp and several state political figures of stock fraud. The federal agency claimed that several high state officials had been bribed to push banking legislation favored by Sharp. The suit alleged that Sharp arranged for the state officials to make quick profits by buying and selling stock in his National Bankers' Life Insurance Company. It was alleged that Sharp's bank lent the politicians the money for those deals. House Speaker Gus Mutscher, Jr., and two of his aides were convicted of conspiring to accept bribes and the fallout ruined the careers of several other politicians.

Frank Sharp was granted probation and immunity from further prosecution when he pleaded guilty to making a false bank entry and dealing in unregistered stock and agreed to give testimony against the others. The scandal caused a run on his bank. It closed and Sharp lost control of his Sharpstown empire.

The Hyatt Regency Hotel opened at Louisiana and Dallas and work started on the Pennzoil building in 1972.

The Houston Independent School District established the Houston Community College system in 1972. The system offered classes mostly at night and mostly in the Houston School District's buildings in the beginning. The Community College now has several buildings of its own and it offers classes also in many of the Houston schools and in the Cypress-Fairbanks, Fort Bend, Alief and Katy districts.

The port began a major expansion of its Bayport Division in 1972 and oilman George Mitchell started work on his new town at the Woodlands on the North Freeway. Mitchell estimated an ultimate investment of $3 billion.

Water pollution was getting a lot of attention in 1972 and the Houston Ship Channel was mentioned more than once as possibly the filthiest body of water in the country.

The Houston Independent School District has turned the old San Jacinto High School building over to the Houston Community College. It was on this same campus, at Holman and San Jacinto, that the school district started the college that became the University of Houston. Walter Cronkite was a student here when this was a high school.

Above: *The simplest way to get a view of the port and the channel industrial complex is to drive across the bridge on the 610 Loop. There is another high bridge lower down the channel. It is a toll bridge. This one is free.*

Left: *Ships from all over the world find the latest in cargo handling equipment here.*

Bottom: Visitors may tour the ship channel in the Port Authority's comfortable yacht, Sam Houston. *Reservations are necessary. They may be arranged by calling 225-4044.*

Opposite: *There are steel mills and grain elevators along the channel too, but tank farms, refineries and petrochemical plants dominate the channel banks.*

The city was identified as the biggest single polluter. Inadequate and overloaded sewage treatment plants were the reason. The city started work on an enormous new sewage treatment plant on the channel at 69th Street and stopped issuing new building permits in areas where the sanitary sewer system was not adequate.

The space base at Clear Lake took a new name in 1973 and became the Lyndon B. Johnson Manned Spacecraft Center. The legislature approved a bill allowing the creation of a Metropolitan Transit Authority, but voters in Houston turned down the idea and the city took over operation of the bankrupt bus system.

The first bridge over the ship channel was completed in 1973 as the final link in the 610 Loop System.

Mayor Louie Welch decided not to run for a sixth term after serving an unprecedented five consecutive terms. Former mayor Roy Hofheinz's son Fred was elected mayor in 1974 and Welch was elected president of the Houston Chamber of Commerce. Fred Hofheinz served two terms as mayor. Real estate developer Jim McConn succeeded him in 1978.

The Chamber of Commerce calculated in 1974 that new people were moving to Houston at the rate of 55,000 a year.

The Two Houston Center building was completed in Houston Center that year.

The only passenger train still using Union Station was switched to the Southern Pacific Station in 1974 and Union Station was closed.

The new City Library Building was completed in the Civic Center in 1975 and the Summit Arena opened in Greenway Plaza. The Summit was built with the proceeds from a city revenue bond issue on land donated by developer Kenneth Schnitzer. The city owns the building and leases it to an operating company in an arrangement similar to the one between the county and the Houston Sports Association. The Summit is the home of the Houston Rockets of the National Basketball Association. The Rockets came to Houston in 1971. They had no regular place to play their games until the Summit opened. The Summit was also the home of the Houston Aeros hockey team until it folded in 1977.

The Houston Rodeo was the biggest in the world by 1975. The Livestock Show and Rodeo moved from the Sam Houston Coliseum to the Astrodome in 1966 and attendance increased dramatically. Houstonians voted in 1975 to allow the sale of liquor by the drink and the restaurant and convention businesses got a big boost.

The One Houston Center building in Houston Center was completed in 1977. The Cadillac-Fairview Company bought half interest in Houston Center the following year. Work also started in 1977 on the First International Bank tower, where the Memorial Hospital had been.

The National Women's Conference was held in Houston in November, 1977. It was part of the observance of International Women's Year and it was the biggest women's meeting ever held in America. Former Congresswoman Bella Abzug was in the chair and the delegates resolved among other things that the Equal Rights Amendment

Above: *The Ringling Brothers, Barnum and Bailey Circus played in the Astrodome once when the dome was new. The place was too big. Most of the audience was sitting higher than the high-wire performers. The circus now plays in the Summit Arena, where the Rockets play basketball. The ice shows use the Summit and most of the rock concerts do, too. Elvis Presley gave his last Houston performance here.*

Right: *There is a Civil Defense shelter and Emergency Operating Center under the Music Hall downtown. These Civil Defense employees work here regularly. They would be joined by the mayor and top city and county, police and fire officials if the city ever were attacked.*

ought to be ratified.

British Caledonian Airways started direct service between Houston and London in 1977. The transit system established the first Park and Ride Service on the Gulf Freeway and started planning contraflow lanes for buses on the freeways. Houston voters approved the creation of a Metropolitan Transit Authority in 1978 to take over the bus system. They also approved a sales tax of one percent to pay for improvements in the system. Contraflow service began on the North Freeway in 1979. It worked better than most people had expected. There was only one fatal accident in the first three years.

The Chamber of Commerce reported that 539 energy companies had headquarters in Houston by 1978.

Tranquility Park in the Civic Center was completed in 1979 and the city council granted five cable television companies the right to wire the city for cable TV.

The port reported a new record of 112,056,767 tons of cargo handled during 1979.

Work began that year on the Texas Commerce Tower. The value of building permits issued by the city for the year 1979 went over $2 billion for the first time. Almost three times as much office space was built in the 1970s as was built in the 1960s.

The city annexed another 102 square miles in the 70s and the population increased by 38 percent. The number of vehicles increased from 1,098,985 in 1970 to 2,000,000 in 1979 and mobility became the chief concern of the city's leaders. The Chamber of Commerce's Houston Area Oxidants study was completed in 1979. It was described as the only detailed study ever made of the quality of Houston's air. The study concluded that air pollution is not a threat to health here. Chamber officials hope the study will help the city fend off Environmental Protection Agency moves to limit industrial building permits and restrict the use of motor vehicles.

Voters in 1979 approved a change to the city charter raising the number of council members to 14 and providing that 9 of the council members be elected by districts.

Top: *Building permits reached a record high of $2 billion in Houston in 1979. One reason was that work began on the Texas Commerce Tower, center left, that year.*

Bottom: *Bigger and newer buildings than this one have been torn down to make way for new buildings in downtown Houston, but the old Auditorium Hotel at Texas and Louisiana is being renovated instead. The hotel was built when the old City Auditorium occupied the site across the street now occupied by Jones Hall. There were concerts in the old auditorium, but wrestling was one of the big events and many of the wrestlers stayed here at the Auditorium Hotel. The new owners are looking for a different clientele at the hotel they will call the Lancaster.*

Left: *The banks of Buffalo Bayou are landscaped between the western edge of downtown and River Oaks. But the bayou banks are overgrown with weeds and willows in the downtown area and on the east side. There has been talk for years about turning this neglected part of the bayou into an asset like San Antonio's River Walk. It appears in 1982 that this may be about to happen.*

Below: *Some of the people hoping so are these Mexican-American business and civic leaders. They want to turn the old furniture factory building in the background into a Mexican market. The building is on the bayou at Runnels Street.*

The Census of 1980 showed a population of 1,594,086 for Houston. Only New York, Chicago, Los Angeles and Philadelphia had bigger numbers and by unofficial calculations Houston passed Philadelphia in 1982.

A survey of new office buildings in 1981 revealed that more new office space was built in the suburbs than was built downtown during the preceeding five years. *Houston Magazine* listed 54 suburban office parks, but building continued in the central business district, too. Work was proceeding on the Capital National Plaza in Allen Center, on the First City Tower, on 1010 Lamar and on 801 Travis. Also the old Memorial Professional Building on Louisiana was being demolished to make way for the new Allied Bank Tower. Building permits in 1980 totalled $2.5 billion.

The city bought the old Sharpstown Country Club in 1980 and started converting it to a city park. The city council agreed to make the two blocks bound by Texas Avenue, Smith, Preston and the bayou available for a proposed new Lyric Theater. And there was serious talk about a new convention center east of Main Street.

Work began in 1981 on the Allied Bank Tower, on the new Gulf Building in Houston Center and on the Park in Houston Center. The Meridien Hotel opened in Allen Center, west of Main. The Meridien is a French hotel with an expensive French restaurant. The hotel is operated by Air France.

There has been talk for more than 20 years about beautifying Buffalo Bayou in the downtown area. Plans were finally drawn up in 1981 by the Buffalo Bayou Beautification Association. The Wortham Foundation donated half a million dollars to get work started on the first phase between Interstate-45 and Sabine Street. There will be landscaping and walkways eventually all the way from Shepherd Drive on the west to Hirsch Road on the east.

Gerald Hines started work in 1981 on a new tower for Republic Bank on the block bound by Smith, Capitol, Louisiana and Rusk. Hines bought the Lamar Hotel block, bound by Main, McKinney, Travis and Lamar, but he made

Above: *Views of the spectacular Pennzoil Place, on the right, are going to be severely limited when the structure in the foreground is completed.*

Left: *The block bound by Smith, Rusk, Louisiana and Capitol will be occupied by the Republic Bank Tower, designed by Philip Johnson and being built by Gerald D. Hines. The style is substantially less severe than that of most recent downtown buildings.*

Opposite right: *Hines is also working on a new tower for Transco on South Post Oak near the Galleria.*

Opposite far right: *The Transco Tower will have a glass skin and a mirror finish. It will be the tallest building outside the downtown area.*

no announcement of his plans for the plot.

The Bank of the Southwest announced plans for a new tower on the block immediately west of the present bank building.

Suburban buildings continued to get bigger. American General started work on a new 42-story tower in the American General Center at Allen Parkway and Waugh. Gerald Hines started work on a new building for Transco. The Transco Tower will be 64 floors, the tallest building

outside the downtown area. It is going up off the West Loop next to the Galleria.

The Prudential Insurance Company's PIC subsidiary started work on a new office and commercial center called City West Place. This development is on Westheimer at West Belt, miles beyond the Galleria. The total investment is expected to be around $2 billion.

Building permits issued by the city for the year 1981 topped $3 billion. This is the largest total ever recorded in a single year by any city in America.

The port was again third in the nation in total tonnage handled and first in foreign trade.

The city and the Hermann Hospital Estate finally got around in 1981 to putting up a statue of George Hermann. It is on a landscaped corner of Hermann Park at Fannin and Hermann Drive.

The city election in the fall of 1981 produced something new. Mayor Jim McConn was ousted by City Controller Kathy Whitmire. The first woman ever elected mayor of Houston took office in January, 1982.

The Four Seasons Hotel in Houston Center was completed in April, 1982. Several high-rise condominium buildings were completed in 1981 and 1982. The units were selling very slowly, but developers went right on putting up office buildings. Plans were announced for the 50-story Four Allen Center. Work started on the United Bank Plaza Building at 1415 Louisiana in the same area. Work began early in 1982 on the 1600 Jefferson Building on Smith Street in Cullen Center.

Opposite: *City Controller Kathy Whitmire beat out Mayor Jim McConn and Sheriff Jack Heard in the city election of 1981 to become the first woman ever elected to the office of mayor of Houston. The city council in the first year of her administration approved an ordinance specifying how far buildings must be set back from major thoroughfares. The ordinance was engineered by Councilwoman Eleanor Tinsley. It is about as close as the city government has ever come to telling builders how to build — and about as close as it is likely to come.*

Top right: *No one can say what Houston would look like if the city had adopted zoning and strict building regulations in the beginning, but there is a good chance that Smith Street will soon be the best looking commercial thoroughfare in America. Smith will be lined with mostly new and good-looking buildings for 17 blocks, from the bayou to Pierce Street when the Allied Bank Tower here and the nearby Republic Bank Tower are finished, when the 1600 Smith Building and Four Allen Center are completed to the south and when the proposed Lyric Theater is built at the north end.*

Right: *This statue of George Hermann stands on the southeast corner of the park Hermann donated and it faces the hospital his money built. Herman Park had a free campground for tourists in the 1920s. Some West Texas towns still maintain free campgrounds for travelers. Houston does not.*

Opposite top: *Someone asked Bob Hope on a television talk show what he thought was the prettiest view he had seen and he said he thought it was the view from the Warwick Hotel in Houston. The Warwick is at the junction of South Main and Montrose. It was an old apartment hotel when the late oilman John Mecom bought it in 1952 for less than $2 million. Mecom spent nearly $12 million fixing the place up and furnishing it with rare antiques.*

Opposite center left: *The Houston Fire Department has turned old Fire Station Number Seven into a museum. The exhibits include this old water tower. It was the first one the department ever had. It was drawn by horses originally. The engine was added later. Number Seven Station was built at Milam and McIlhenny in 1899. The Houston Police Department is also developing a museum at the police academy on Aldine-Westfield Road at Rankin.*

Opposite center right: *Dominique de Menil and her late husband, John, bought this metal sculpture in the 1960s. They wanted to give it to the city and have it displayed in some prominent place as a memorial to Dr. Martin Luther King. Some city council members objected to the sculpture and some objected to the idea of a memorial to Dr. King. So the de Menils installed the sculpture on the grounds of the Rothko Chapel they built at Sul Ross and Yupon near the University of St. Thomas. The chapel is a non-denominational place of worship and meditation* decorated with oil paintings done especially for the chapel by the late Mark Rothko. Mrs. de Menil is planning a museum in the same vicinity to house her extensive art collection. She inherited the Schlumberger well servicing fortune.*

Opposite bottom: *Very little was happening before 1957 along Farm Road 1960 in northwest Harris County. The road was usually called Jack Rabbit Road then. People started moving into the area after Jackie Burke and Jimmie Demeret built the Champions Gulf Club. The FM 1960 area has a population now of about 200,000 and it is sure to be annexed to Houston shortly.*

Top: *An eccentric named Jeff McKissack bought this place at 2401 Munger in the 1960s. McKissick was very partial to oranges and he turned his property into a showplace. All the decorations are tributes to the orange. McKissack conceived and built all of them himself. Some critics rank his Orange Show with folk art masterpieces like the Watts Tower in Las Angeles. McKissack died in 1980 at the age of 78. Some of his fans started a foundation and raised money to buy and preserve his Orange Show.*

Top left: *There is no sure way to beat the frustrations of Houston's traffic. But some Houstonians have found they can climb off the freeways when the traffic stops moving if they have a vehicle with four-wheel drive.*

Center: *Houstonians so minded can join just about any of the city's clubs if they have the money and members to sponsor them. The Bayou Club is the most exclusive. It is said the only way to become a member here is to be born one. The clubhouse is on the edge of Memorial Park. The Houston Polo Club plays regular games in the spring and fall on a field near the Bayou Club. The field is visible from I-10 West, but it is not open to the public. Only members and their guests are admitted.*

Bottom: *Chamber of Commerce President Louie Welch does not think it is inevitable that Houston will continue to grow at the rate it has grown in the past. He does think it is pretty likely. Welch says the growth has occurred because people find economic opportunities here and an agreeable place to live. He says as long as they continue to find these, people will continue to come here.*

Opposite: *Houston looked unfinished when I first saw it. It looks unfinished still. Buildings under construction are a reassuring sign that the city is still growing. This growth rate is not as thrilling as it was when Barney McCasland arrived to make the population an even one million. There have not been any more celebrations like that one, but not many people would want the growth to stop.*

The city had workmen busy at Hobby Airport, renovating the old terminal and building a new parking garage. The city and the Metropolitan Transit Authority both endorsed a Regional Mobility Plan put forward by the Transportation Committee of the Chamber of Commerce. The plan calls for expanding the freeways, the major thoroughfares and the transit system and adding some rail lines and toll roads over the next 15 years. The planners think the proposed improvements will restore mobility in Houston to what it was in the middle 1970s. Traffic congestion has risen to the top of the city's list of problems.

Some of the city's rich and mighty still meet in the afternoons in Suite 8-F. Many of the old crowd are gone. New people have replaced them. But George Brown is still there. Louie Welch says one of Houston's great strengths has been the dynamic flexibility of the establishment. He says the establishment in Houston has always been open to new people and new ideas. Whatever the establishment, the Chamber of Commerce and the city government have attempted has always been accomplished. Maybe they can untangle the traffic jam created by the success of their other endeavors. If they cannot, the city will be strangled before the developers get it built. ■

PHOTO CREDITS

The color photographs for this book were made by Fred Edison with the exception of the NASA photograph on page 58. The black and white photographs were made by the author except for those listed below. The author and publisher wish to express their gratitude to these individuals and organizations for permitting the reproduction of photographs from their collections:

ABC TV, 35 (lower)
Associated Press, 27
CBS TV, 35 (upper)
Century Development, Inc., 37 (lower)
Channel 13, 18
Edward Bourdon, 2, 10, 15, 147, 165, 167
Gary James, 167
Gerald D. Hines Interests, 37 (upper), 200, 216, 217
Houston Chamber of Commerce by James R. LaCombe, 191
Houston Chronicle, 15 (right), 28, 31, 121 (lower), 150
Houston Fire Department, 112 (middle)
Houston Lighting and Power Company, 97
Houston Magazine, 179
Metropolitan Research Center, Houston Public Library, 10 (lower),
    11, 12 (lower), 64 (upper right), 64 (upper left), 64 (lower right),
    67 (upper right), 67 (lower), 69, 70, 73, 78, 82, 84 (all), 90, 97, 99
    (lower), 100, 104 (upper), 104 (lower), 108, 110, 111, 112 (upper),
    112 (lower), 114, 120, 122, 123, 125 (upper), 126, 128 (both), 129,
    141 (lower), 146 (upper), 146 (lower), 149 (all), 151 (upper left), 179
Port of Houston Authority, 143 (upper)
Prince Family, 7
Rice University, 77
St. Joseph's Hospital, 99 (upper)
Sam Houston High School Library, 144, 145 (upper)
San Jacinto Museum of History, Cecil Thompson Collection, courtesy
    Metropolitan Research Center, Houston Public Library, 6, 8, 101,
    117, 140 (lower), 142
Southwestern Bell, 94 (upper)
Spaw-Glass, 102
Texas Commerce Bank by John Van Beekum, 140 (upper)
Texas Heart Institute, 199
Texas Southern University Library, 22 (lower)
Tijerina Family, 22 (center)

INDEX

Bold type indicates the location of a related photograph.

ACKNOWLEDGEMENTS

We are indebted to Doris Glasser and the staff of the Texas and Local History Room of the Houston Public Library for assisting us in our research.

Some of the publications we found helpful and worthy of recommendation to readers wishing more information are:

Albert Thomas, Late a Representative from Texas: U.S. Government Printing Office.

Architectural Survey: Southwest Center for Urban Research and the School of Architecture, Rice University.

Big Town, Big Money: editorial staff, *Houston Business Journal.*

Blood and Money: Thomas Thompson.

Corduroy Road: Wallace Davis.

Decisive Years for Houston: Marvin Hurley.

Eagle, The, Autobiography of Santa Anna: edited by Ann Fears Crawford.

Grand Huckster, The: Edgar W. Ray.

Handbook of Texas: Texas State Historical Association.

Houston, A History: David G. McComb.

Houston, A History and Guide: American Guide Series Writers' Program, Work Projects Administration.

Houston Review, The: Houston Metropolitan Research Center, Houston Public Library.

Houston, Super City of the Southwest: William Shelton and Ann Kennedy.

Houston, The Once and Future City: George Fuermann.

Howard, The Amazing Mr. Hughes: Noah Dietrich and Bob Thomas.

Illustrated 20th Century Deep Water Edition of Houston, Texas, Progressive City of the Empire State: W.W. Dexter.

Jesse H. Jones, The Man and The Statesman: Bascom N. Timmons.

John H. Freeman and His Friends, A Story of the Texas Medical Center and How it Began: N. Don Macon.

Joseph Stephen Cullinan: John O. King.

Lagerstromia, Handbook/Checklist, A Guide to Crapemyrtle Cultivars: Donald R. Egolf and Ann O. Andrick.

Last American City, The: Douglas Milbourn.

Life and Literary Remains of Sam Houston: William Carey Crane.

Port of Houston, The: Marilyn McAdams Sibley.

Raven: The: Marquis James.

Right Stuff, The: Tom Wolfe.

Texas 1874: Edward King and J. Wells Champney.

Texas, The Country and its Men: L.E. Daniell.

Thumb Nail History of the City of Houston, Texas: Dr. S.O. Young.

True Stories of Old Houston and Houstonians: Dr. S.O. Young.

Two Thousand Miles in Texas on Horseback: N.A. Taylor.

Visit to Texas in 1831, A: (author unknown).

William Bollaert's Texas: edited by W. Eugene Hallon and Ruth Lapham Butler.

William Marsh Rice and His Institute: Andrew Forest Muir.

Yellow Rose of Texas, The: Martha Ann Turner.